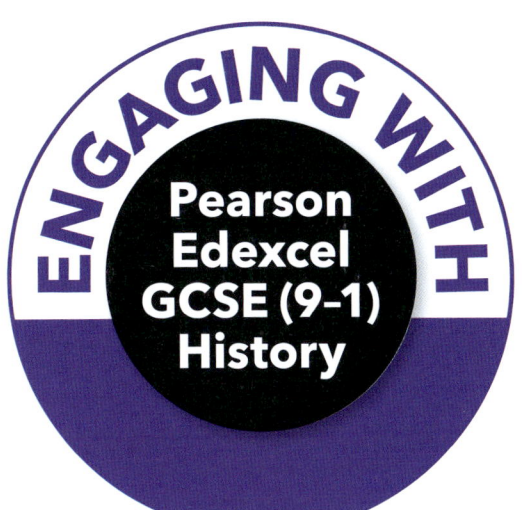

CRIME AND PUNISHMENT IN BRITAIN c1000–PRESENT

AND WHITECHAPEL, c1870–c1900

JEMMA TAPPENDEN

Series Consultants:
Dale Banham & Sam Slater

The Publishers would like to thank the following for permission to reproduce copyright material.

Photo credits

p. 8t © Chetham's Library / Bridgeman Images; **p. 8b** © Pictorial Press Ltd / Alamy Stock Photo; **p. 9t** © Chroma Collection / Alamy Stock Photo; **p. 9m** © PA Images / Alamy Stock Photo; **p. 10l** © The Print Collector / Alamy Stock Photo; **p. 10tm** © Mark Richardson / Alamy Stock Photo; **p. 10bm** © Heritage Image Partnership Ltd / Alamy Stock Photo; **p. 10r** © British Library archive / Bridgeman Images; **p. 14** © Chetham's Library / Bridgeman Images; **p. 19** © Art Collection 2 / Alamy Stock Photo; **p. 20** © The Reading Room / Alamy Stock Photo; **p. 23** © World History Archive / Alamy Stock Photo; **p. 25** © Geoffrey Morgan / Alamy Stock Photo; **p. 30** © Pictorial Press Ltd / Alamy Stock Photo; **p. 32** © Colin Waters / Alamy Stock Photo; **p. 35** © Chronicle / Alamy Stock Photo; **p. 36** © Historic Images / Alamy Stock Photo; **p. 38** © Walker Art Library / Alamy Stock Photo; **p. 40** © Heritage Image Partnership Ltd / Alamy Stock Photo; **p. 41** © Heritage Image Partnership Ltd / Alamy Stock Photo; **p. 42** © Archivist / Alamy Stock Photo; **p. 43** © Chronicle / Alamy Stock Photo; **p. 44** © ART Collection / Alamy Stock Photo; **p. 45** © The Print Collector / Alamy Stock Photo; **p. 50** © Chronicle / Alamy Stock Photo; **p. 51** © World History Archive / Alamy Stock Photo; **p. 53** © Pictorial Press Ltd / Alamy Stock Photo; **p. 54** © Chronicle / Alamy Stock Photo; **p. 57** © Pictorial Press Ltd / Alamy Stock Photo; **p. 59** © Chronicle / Alamy Stock Photo; **p. 60** © Niday Picture Library / Alamy Stock Photo; **p. 61t** © Chronicle / Alamy Stock Photo; **p. 61b** © National Archives; **p. 65** © The Trustees of the British Museum; **p. 67** © World History Archive / Alamy Stock Photo; **p. 68** © Chronicle / Alamy Stock Photo; **p. 69** © Chronicle / Alamy Stock Photo; **p. 70** © National Archives; **p. 71** © Chroma Collection / Alamy Stock Photo; **p. 78** © Kurt Hutton/Picture Post / Hulton Archive / Getty Images; **p. 81** © Trinity Mirror / Mirrorpix / Alamy Stock Photo; **p. 83t** © James Boardman Archive / Alamy Stock Photo; **p. 83b** © London Borough of Lambeth; **p. 84** © Dario Earl / Alamy Stock Photo; **p. 86** © Benjamin John / Alamy Stock Photo; **p. 89** © Metropolitan Police Authority / Mary Evans; **p. 91** Ankle tag; **p. 92** © The National Archives; **p. 93** © PA Photos / TopFoto; **p. 94** © Keystone Press / Alamy Stock Photo; **p. 95l** © PA Images / Alamy Stock Photo; **p. 95r** © PA Images / Alamy Stock Photo; **p. 96** © Daily Herald Archive / National Science & Media Museum / SSPL via Getty Images; **p. 97** © Popperfoto via Getty Images / Getty Images; **p. 98** © piemags / RTM / Alamy Stock Photo; **p. 99** © Imperial War Museum; **p. 105** Cover of *The Five: The Untold Lives of the Women Killed by Jack the Ripper* by Hallie Rubenhold © Transworld Publishers Ltd; **p. 106** © Birkbeck History Dept / Public Domain via Wikimedia Commons; **p. 107** © National Archives; **p. 109** © Photo 12 / Alamy Stock Photo; **p. 110** Original: Charles Booth's Labour and Life of the People. Volume 1: East London (London: Macmillan, 1889) via Wikimedia Commons/Public Domain; **p. 111** © Pictorial Press Ltd / Alamy Stock Photo; **p. 113** © Royal Holloway, University of London / Bridgeman Images; **p. 114** © Wikimedia / Public Domain; **p. 117** © National Railway Museum / Science & Society Picture Library; **p. 118** © Trinity Mirror / Mirrorpix / Alamy Stock Photo; **p. 119 and 132** © Cornell University – PJ Mode Collection of Persuasive Cartography; **p. 121** © Chronicle / Alamy Stock Photo; **p. 123** © The Print Collector / Alamy Stock Photo; **p. 128** From the British Library archive / Bridgeman Images

Although every effort has been made to ensure that website addresses are correct at time of going to press, Hachette Learning cannot be held responsible for the content of any website mentioned in this book. It is sometimes possible to find a relocated web page by typing in the address of the home page for a website in the URL window of your browser.

Hachette UK's policy is to use papers that are natural, renewable and recyclable products and made from wood grown in well-managed forests and other controlled sources. The logging and manufacturing processes are expected to conform to the environmental regulations of the country of origin.

To order, please visit www.hachettelearning.com or contact Customer Service at education@hachette.co.uk / +44 (0)1235 827827.

ISBN: 978 1 3983 8925 0

© Jemma Tappendale 2025

First published in 2025 by Hachette Learning,
An Hachette UK Company
Carmelite House
50 Victoria Embankment
London EC4Y 0DZ

www.hachettelearning.com

The authorised representative in the EEA is Hachette Ireland, 8 Castlecourt Centre, Dublin 15, D15 XTP3, Ireland (email: info@hbgi.ie)

Impression number 10 9 8 7 6 5 4 3 2 1

Year   2029 2028 2027 2026 2025

All rights reserved. Apart from any use permitted under UK copyright law, no part of this publication may be reproduced or transmitted in any form or by any means, electronic or mechanical, including photocopying and recording, or held within any information storage and retrieval system, without permission in writing from the publisher or under licence from the Copyright Licensing Agency Limited. Further details of such licences (for reprographic reproduction) may be obtained from the Copyright Licensing Agency Limited, www.cla.co.uk

Cover photo © Lebrecht Music & Arts / Alamy Stock Photo

Typeset in India by Aptara

Printed in Glasgow by Bell & Bain Ltd

A catalogue record for this title is available from the British Library.

CONTENTS

Introduction 4

1 c1000–c1500: Crime and punishment in medieval England 14

Connect and Engage – William I 14
- **1.1** The nature and changing definitions of crime in medieval England 15
- **1.2** The role of the authorities and local communities in law enforcement in medieval England 18
- **1.3** The nature of punishment in medieval England 22
- **1.4** Case study: The influence of the Church on crime and punishment in the early thirteenth century 24
- **1.5** Medieval period review 26
- **1.6** Medieval period exam practice 28

2 c1500–c1700: Crime and punishment in early modern England 30

Connect and Engage – Guy Fawkes 30
- **2.1** Change and continuity in definitions of crime in early modern England 31
- **2.2** The role of the authorities and local communities in law enforcement c1500–c1700 38
- **2.3** Punishment in early modern England 40
- **2.4** Case study 1: The Gunpowder Plot 42
- **2.5** Case study 2: Matthew Hopkins 44
- **2.6** Early modern period review 46
- **2.7** Early modern period exam practice 48

3 c1700–c1900: Crime and punishment in eighteenth- and nineteenth-century Britain 50

Connect and Engage – Michael Barrett 50
- **3.1** Understanding the eighteenth and nineteenth centuries 51
- **3.2** Changing definitions of criminal activity c1700–c1900 52
- **3.3** The nature of law enforcement c1700–c1900 58
- **3.4** Changing views on the purpose of punishment c1700–c1900 64
- **3.5** Case study 1: Pentonville prison 68
- **3.6** Case study 2: The reforms of Robert Peel 71
- **3.7** Eighteenth- and nineteenth-century Britain review 74
- **3.8** Eighteenth- and nineteenth-century Britain exam practice 76

4 c1900–present: Crime and punishment in modern Britain 78

Connect and Engage – Violet Van der Elst 78
- **4.1** The nature and changing definitions of criminal activity 79
- **4.2** New definitions of crime 82
- **4.3** The nature of law enforcement c1900–present 86
- **4.4** Punishment c1900–present 90
- **4.5** Case study 1: The Derek Bentley case and its significance for the abolition of the death penalty 96
- **4.6** Case study 2: The treatment of conscientious objectors in the First and Second World Wars 98
- **4.7** Modern Britain review 100
- **4.8** Modern Britain exam practice 101

5 Whitechapel, c1870–c1900: crime, policing and the inner city 104

- **5.1** How do we know about crime and policing in Whitechapel, c1870–c1900? 104
- **5.2** The local context: Whitechapel c1870–c1900 106
- **5.3** The inhabitants of Whitechapel 116
- **5.4** The national and regional context 120
- **5.5** The organisation of policing in Whitechapel 122
- **5.6** Investigative policing in Whitechapel 126
- **5.7** Whitechapel c1870–c1900 review 130
- **5.8** Whitechapel c1870–c1900 exam practice 132

Glossary 134
Index 136

Introduction to the thematic study and historic environment

0.1 Your exam

What is assessed and how

The GCSE course that you are following is made up of four different studies.

	Paper 1: Thematic study and historic environment	Paper 2: Period study and British depth study	Paper 3: Modern depth study
What is assessed?	**Section A: Historic environment** This focuses on the relationship between a place and historical events and developments.	**Option P: Period study** This focuses on a wider world topic over a period of at least 50 years.	This focuses on the complexity of a historical society or situation. The interplay of different aspects of history is considered.
	Section B: Thematic study This focuses on change and continuity across a long sweep of history, from the medieval period to the present day.	**Option B: British depth study** This focuses on a period of British history over a short period of time (less than 40 years).	
How is it assessed?	Written exam: 1 hour 20 minutes 30% of your GCSE (52 marks) **Section A** – 3 compulsory questions (16 marks) **Section B** – 2 compulsory questions and 1 from a choice of 2 (36 marks)	Written exam: 1 hour 50 minutes 40% of your GCSE (64 marks) **Period study** – 2 compulsory questions and 2 from a choice of 3 (32 marks) **British depth study** – 2 compulsory questions and 1 from a choice of 2 (32 marks)	Written exam: 1 hour and 30 minutes 30% of your GCSE (52 marks) **Section A** – 1 compulsory question and 1 from a choice of 2 (16 marks) **Section B** – 4 compulsory questions (36 marks)

This book prepares you for **Paper 1: Crime and punishment in Britain, c1000–present and Whitechapel c1870–c1900: crime, policing and the inner city**.

It focuses on how crime and punishment changed in Britain over a long period of time. You will study:

- how key features in the changes to definitions of crime and the nature of punishment were linked with the key features of society in Britain across different time periods
- the causes and consequences of the changes that took place in crime and punishment
- the significance of key developments, individuals and events
- the nature and process of change. This will involve understanding patterns of change, trends and turning points, and the influence of factors encouraging or inhibiting change within periods and across themes in crime and punishment.

Period and theme	Key content	Review pages
1 Crime and punishment in medieval England, c1000–c1500	<ul><li>Medieval definitions of crime against authority, the person, property</li><li>Changing definitions of crime after the Norman Conquest</li><li>The role of local communities in medieval law enforcement</li><li>The nature and purpose of punishment</li><li>Case study: The influence of the Church on crime and punishment</li></ul>	Pages 26–27
2 Crime and punishment in early modern England, c1500–c1700	<ul><li>Change and continuity in the definitions of crime</li><li>Changes to the role of the local community in law enforcement</li><li>Continuity in the nature and purpose of punishment</li><li>Case studies: The Gunpowder Plot and Matthew Hopkins</li></ul>	Pages 46–47
3 Crime and punishment in eighteenth- and nineteenth-century Britain, c1700–c1900	<ul><li>Changing definitions of criminal activity</li><li>New approaches to law enforcement</li><li>New attitudes to the nature and purpose of punishment</li><li>Case studies: Pentonville prison and the reforms of Robert Peel</li></ul>	Pages 74–75
4 Crime and punishment in modern Britain, c1900–present	<ul><li>New definitions of crime in the twentieth and twenty-first centuries</li><li>Modern-day policing</li><li>The abolition of the death penalty and alternatives to prison</li><li>Case studies: The case of Derek Bentley and the treatment of conscientious objectors in the First and Second World Wars</li></ul>	Page 100
5 Whitechapel, c1870–c1900	<ul><li>The local context of Whitechapel, including problems with overcrowding and housing</li><li>Provisions for the poor</li><li>The impact of migration on Whitechapel</li><li>Policing and the problems of investigating the Ripper murders</li></ul>	Pages 130–31

Revision Tip

Break down your revision into manageable chunks of content
- This book is organised into five parts that reflect the parts of the specification.
- At the end of each part of the course, make sure you review and revise what you have just covered.
- The 'Exam Practice', 'Recall Challenge' and 'Review' features will help you do this.

How the thematic study will be examined

> **Exam Tip**
>
> **Take time to understand the question**
> You should always spend time making sure you identify the focus of the question and planning your approach **before** you start to write your answer.

Type of question	Guidance	Marks	Writing time	Advice and practice
Section A: The historic environment: Whitechapel, c1870–1800: crime, policing and the inner city					
These questions require you to analyse and evaluate historical sources (contemporary to the period).				
1a/b a Describe one feature of … b Describe one feature of …	Focus on the question – identify a feature and then support with a sentence of historical information. Repeat for question 1b.	2 + 2	6 minutes	Pages 108, 114 and 129
2a How useful are Sources A and B for an enquiry into …	The sources could be visual or written. They will relate to an aspect of the enquiry in the question. Focus on how the sources are useful. Use the content of the source, the provenance of the source and your contextual knowledge to evaluate the usefulness of the sources.	8	12 minutes	Pages 109, 114, 119, 129 and 132
2b How could you follow up Source A/B to find out more about …	Identify a detail from the content of the source linked to the enquiry in the question. Write a question that will provide you with more information for the enquiry. Identify a contemporary source and make it specific to the enquiry. Check that it will have the answer to your question. Explain how the source will answer your question.	4	6 minutes	Pages 125, 129 and 133

> **Revision Tip**
>
> **Make exam practice part of your revision**
> Exam Tips give you step-by-step guidance on how to tackle each type of question. Effective revision is not just learning the content. You need to understand what each type of question is asking you to think about in the exam and to practise delivering it.

	Type of question	Guidance	Marks	Writing time	Advice and practice
Section B: Thematic study: Crime and punishment in Britain, c1000–present These questions focus on second-order concepts such as continuity, change, cause, consequence, significance, similarity and difference.					
3	Explain one way … similar/different …	Focus on the question – explain a similarity or difference. Support with historical examples from both time periods in the question.	4	6 minutes	Pages 37, 47, 76, 86 and 102
4	Explain why …	Focus on the question and explain why there was change in crime and punishment. Aim to write three paragraphs. Support your answer with at least three aspects of knowledge.	12	18 minutes	Pages 73, 76–77, 85, 91, 97 and 103
5/6	'Statement': How far do you agree?	This is an essay question, requiring you to reach a judgement. Aim to agree with the statement and then disagree with an alternative argument. Support your answer with at least three aspects of knowledge. Make sure that you write a conclusion explaining how far you agree with the statement.	20 (16 + 4 for SPaG)	30 minutes	Pages 28–29, 48, 49, 77 and 103

> **Revision Tip**
>
> **Take responsibility**
> Reflect on your strengths and weaknesses. What question types do you struggle with? Spend more time practising the types of question you find most difficult. Use feedback from your teacher to improve your approach.

0.2 The Big Picture: Identify the key questions

Connect and Engage

The period summaries below identify people and events that have shaped crime and punishment in Britain since c1000. They also show the big questions you will cover. However, top history students do not only answer other people's questions, they also ask questions of their own!

As you read each summary, note down your own questions (large or small) about each period.

Part 1: c1000–c1500: Crime and punishment in medieval England, *The impact of the Norman Conquest*

Big question: How far was the Norman Conquest a turning point for crime and punishment in medieval England?

Definitions of criminal activity	The nature of law enforcement and punishment
• **Crime against authority** was the most serious type of crime during the medieval period. Those who threatened the social order, and particularly those who threatened the power and authority of the monarch, were punished severely. • After the **Norman Conquest**, William I introduced new laws such as the Murdrum Law and the **Forest Laws**, which led to new definitions of crime against authority. 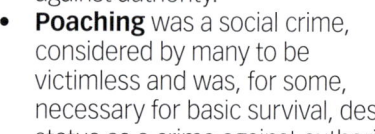 • **Poaching** was a social crime, considered by many to be victimless and was, for some, necessary for basic survival, despite its official status as a crime against authority. • Other definitions of crime included **crimes against the person** and **crimes against property**.	• Medieval punishment aimed to serve as a **deterrent**. In the absence of a police force, deterring criminals from committing crime in the first place was important. • **Retribution** was an important part of punishment. Severe punishments such as the **death penalty** ensured the criminal paid the ultimate price for their crime and served as a deterrent to others. • **Fines** were used for less serious crimes. • The Church had a big influence on crime and punishment, offering **sanctuary** to criminals and **trial by ordeal** to establish innocence or guilt. Tension between the Church and the monarch (who had ultimate responsibility for law and order) grew throughout the period. • Communities were small, so a system of community-based law enforcement was common. This worked on the principle of **collective responsibility** – all members of the community had a responsibility to uphold and enforce the law.

Part 2: c1500–c1700: Crime and punishment in early modern England, *A period of religious instability*

Big question: To what extent did religion influence attitudes towards crime and punishment in early modern England?

Definitions of criminal activity	The nature of law enforcement and punishment
• There was little change in the definition of crimes against the person or property. • **Guy Fawkes** and his fellow conspirators were found guilty of **treason** for their failed attempt to blow up parliament in the Gunpowder Plot.  • **Heresy** became a serious crime at a time when religious division and tension were at an all-time high. • There was a huge increase in witch trials as a result of new definitions of **witchcraft** as a crime, which were fuelled by religious paranoia within communities and by the authorities. • **Vagabondage** emerged as a crime after an increase in unemployment and homelessness.	• **Deterrence** and **retribution** continued to be the main aims of punishment in the early modern period. • **Capital punishment** remained the most frequently used punishment for serious crimes, with executions carried out in public. • In 1688 the list of capital crimes (punishable by death) was increased to 50 crimes. This was the beginning of a period which became known as the **Bloody Code**. • **Transportation** was introduced as an alternative to the death penalty. • **Houses of correction** (early prisons) were opened for less serious crimes such as vagrancy. • Communities still played a role in law enforcement, but growing populations led to the introduction of **town watchmen**. • The Tudors removed any remaining influence the Church had on law enforcement, such as **benefit of clergy**.

Part 3: c1700–c1900: Crime and punishment in eighteenth- and nineteenth-century Britain, *A revolution in policing*

Big question: How did Robert Peel revolutionise the nature of law enforcement and punishment?

Definitions of criminal activity	The nature of law enforcement and punishment
<ul><li>An industrial revolution changed the way that people worked and lived. Increased poverty and poor standards of living led to an increase in crimes such as **theft**, which were sometimes simply the result of trying to survive.</li><li>The **Tolpuddle Martyrs** were transported to Australia as authorities became increasingly concerned about trade unions and workers looking to improve their pay and conditions.</li><li>There was an increase in crimes such as **smuggling** and **poaching**, which many still viewed as social crimes.</li></ul> 	<ul><li>Concerns grew throughout the period that **public execution** was no longer an effective deterrent. In 1868, executions were moved to within prison walls, no longer carried out in front of a public audience.</li><li>**Transportation** as a punishment was **abolished**.</li><li>**Prisons** became a much more popular and cost-effective way of punishing criminals, but there was concern over conditions within them. Campaigners such as **John Howard** and **Elizabeth Fry** worked to bring these concerns to the attention of the government so that improvements could be made.</li><li>Brothers **John and Henry Fielding** established the **Bow Street Runners**, a small group of men who policed the area of London around Bow Street.</li><li>**Robert Peel** introduced **penal reform**, which brought the Bloody Code to an end. His **1823 Gaols Act** addressed many of the concerns raised by Fry and, in 1829, he took the **Metropolitan Police Act** through parliament – leading to the first government-backed professional **police force** in London.</li></ul>

Part 4: c1900–present: Crime and punishment in modern Britain, *Modern-day attitudes to crime, punishment and policing*

Big question: How have public attitudes to crime and punishment changed since c1900?

Definitions of criminal activity	The nature of law enforcement and punishment
<ul><li>**Technology** has changed the way that criminals can operate. It has led to new ways of committing crime, such as identity theft and scamming. But it has also impacted the nature of what is targeted by thieves, who often focus on highly priced technology such as cars and mobile devices.</li><li>There have been changes to definitions of criminal activity throughout the twentieth and twenty-first centuries, to include **driving offences**, hate crime, **race crime** and **drug crimes**.</li></ul>	<ul><li>**Science and technology** have also had a huge impact on the effectiveness of policing. **Forensic science** such as **fingerprinting** and **DNA** testing has led to more criminal convictions and the police have made use of technology such as cars, radios and computers to track and catch criminals.</li><li>The **Derek Bentley** case caused a public outcry. The nineteen-year-old was hanged for the murder of a police officer. His case is controversial because of his learning disabilities and the fact that he did not pull the trigger of the gun that killed the officer.</li><li>**Public attitudes** have had a huge impact on punishment. During the mid-twentieth century, capital punishment was abolished in Britain, partly because of public attitudes and media coverage.</li><li>**Rehabilitation** became the main purpose of punishment, with prisoners offered access to education programmes to help them prepare for life after prison.</li></ul>

Part 5: Whitechapel, c1870–1900: Crime, policing and the inner city

Big question: What can we learn from sources about the people, crimes and policing of the Whitechapel area of London?

- Whitechapel was in the poor quarter of London's East End. **Poverty** and **crime** were significant aspects of its environment.
- Poverty, crime and **anti-social behaviour** such as alcoholism were often linked in Whitechapel. Some of its poorest residents committed 'survival' crimes such as theft or prostitution.
- Whitechapel was a maze of narrow cobbled streets featuring **rookeries** and **lodging houses** where the poor lived. This made the area harder to police.
- **H Division** of the Metropolitan Police Force was responsible for the policing of Whitechapel.
- In 1888 the **Jack the Ripper** murders shook Whitechapel. The police were heavily criticised by both the media and local residents for failing to catch the killer.

0.3 Factors that help to explain change and continuity in crime and punishment

Research & Record

What factors influenced the history of crime and punishment?

Over time, definitions of criminal activity and the nature of law enforcement and punishment have changed significantly. Today we might be horrified at the thought of a criminal being subject to public execution as a punishment for stealing. But there was a time when the authorities believed that this was the most effective way to deter would-be criminals.

So why has crime and punishment changed so much over time? That's what this course is all about.

The cards on page 11 show the main factors that have affected crime and punishment. Pictures A–D below show types of punishment during different periods. Which time period does each image show?

1. Can you match one factor from page 11 to each picture?
2. Look back at the Big picture on pages 8 and 9. What factors can you see influencing crime and punishment in each period?
3. Make a large copy of a table like this to record your research. Keep this table and add to it throughout your course. Make sure you provide evidence to support your answers.

Period	Factors that influenced developments	Evidence
c1000–c1500	The role of the Church	The Church offered criminals sanctuary which increased tension between the Church and monarch.
c1500–c1700		
c1700–c1900		
c1900–present day		

▲ Picture A

▲ Picture B

▲ Picture C

▲ Picture D

Change and continuity

Throughout this course, you need to look for change and continuity in crime and punishment in Britain. Consider when change or continuity took place. Consider why crime and punishment changed or continued. Begin to reach judgements about how much change and continuity took place.

Change
When definitions of criminal activity and the nature of law enforcement and punishment were different from previously.

Continuity
When definitions of criminal activity and the nature of law enforcement and punishment stayed the same as previously.

Factors affecting crime and punishment

The role of individuals
Individuals have greatly influenced punishment and law enforcement. For example, during the eighteenth and nineteenth centuries, individuals such as John and Henry Fielding and Robert Peel had a huge impact on policing.

The role of the government
In modern crime and punishment, government plays a crucial role. During the nineteenth century, the government passed laws to compel regions across England to introduce their own police forces. Today these police forces work together, sharing information on a national database to tackle crime. The government passes new laws to deal with modern issues, which have seen new measures in the twenty-first century to overcome drug crimes, hate crime and other forms of discrimination.

The role of the Church
The Church has influenced crime, punishment and law enforcement in the past. For example, in the later medieval period, there were clashes between the Church and monarchs over how much influence the Church had in law enforcement. However, in the early modern period the biggest impact of the Church was in definitions of criminal activity, with witchcraft and heresy laws both heavily influenced by religious fear and belief.

Science and technology
Developments in science and technological improvements have transformed crime, punishment and policing in the past 200 years. New equipment and forensic science, such as fingerprinting and DNA testing, have revolutionised the ways in which criminals are caught and brought to justice.

Attitudes in society
Attitudes in society have both encouraged and inhibited change. For example, in the medieval and early modern periods, the public were an important and enthusiastic audience for public execution. However, this changed in the nineteenth century when public execution ended, and by the twentieth century attitudes in society towards the use of the death penalty had changed significantly, contributing to its eventual abolition as a punishment in Britain.

Revision Tip

Factors affecting change and continuity

Questions 4, 5 and 6 in the exam will test your knowledge and understanding of change and continuity in crime and punishment in Britain. You should use the five factors in the boxes above to explain why there was change and continuity. These questions carry a lot of marks and the more care you give to completing this table as you revise, the better able you will be to write good answers.

0.4 Key features: How this book works

The tasks in this book will help you learn what you need to know and how to apply your knowledge to answer exam questions effectively. They are your **'steps to success'**.

Research & Record

This gets your learning into your head in the first place and into your notebook. It will start you thinking in a way that will help you produce good answers to the exam questions.

Each **research question** reflects an issue that examiners will expect you to be an expert on. Complete these tasks, which build an answer to each research question, carefully and neatly because they will become your revision notes. Many tasks use tables. Give yourself room – each table should have its own page in your notebook.

→ If you have gaps in your knowledge, go back to your research notes and the relevant section of this book and make sure that you add anything that is missing so you have covered all the key topics in enough detail.

Summarise

This turns your learning into a **memorable form**. Sometimes we guide you to do this, but mostly it is up to you.

Memory aids are different from your research notes. They use images or diagrams but few words. Most people remember better if something is summarised with both text and visuals.

→ If you cannot remember some of the content you have covered, go back to your research notes and improve or recreate your memory aid.

Connect & Engage

These tasks make you form **connections** between what you have already learned and what you are about to learn.

Apply ▶ Recall Challenge

Prepare yourself for exams by testing yourself on what you have learned.

Quizzes, games and competitions test how much you can remember. They identify your weak spots where you need to spend more time.

Apply ▶ Exam Practice

Continue to prepare for the exam by answering exam-style questions with our Exam Tips to guide you.

Our **practice questions** are like the questions you will be asked in the exam, although none come from actual past papers. You can get real papers from your teacher or the Edexcel website. There are **Exam Tips** for each question type so you know how to approach them.

→ If you did not understand how to approach an exam question, go back to the Exam Tips in this book and re-read them, checking that you fully understand what is required in a good answer to that type of question.

Review

We regularly **review** the **big ideas and concepts**. We also encourage you to **review your own learning**.

Take responsibility
Review your own learning. What areas did you do well on? What areas do you need to improve?

Revision Tips

1. **Don't delay** revision until just before the exam. Revision should be an ongoing process. You need to revisit topics that you have studied regularly. Otherwise, as the graph shows, you will quickly start to forget key information.
2. **Retrieval practice** makes your memory stronger. When you recall what you have previously studied, your brain strengthens connections and makes it easier to recall this information in the future.
3. **Spaced practice** helps you remember for longer! At the end of each topic, we test you, not just on that topic but on previous ones as well. You should regularly return to the Review tasks from previous topics and test your knowledge of 'older material'. As the graph shows, this should improve recall and stop you forgetting.

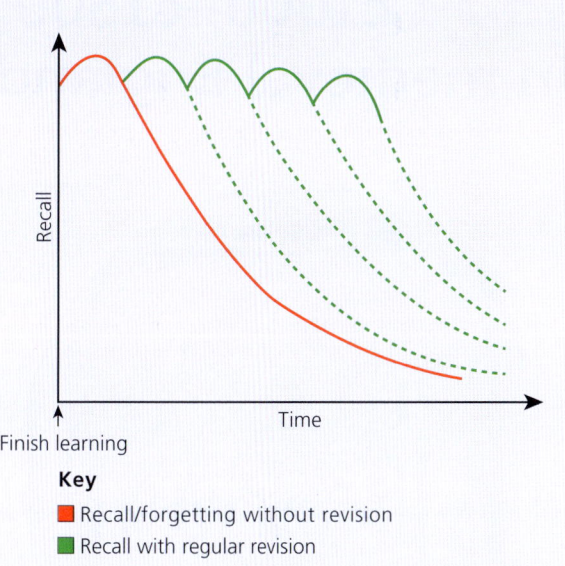

Key
- Recall/forgetting without revision
- Recall with regular revision

Apply ▶ Recall Challenges

Let's start by recalling what you have read in the Big picture on pages 8 and 9.

1 Know the key individuals

Match each person below with the correct description.

Individual	How their work influenced changes in crime and punishment
William I	Campaigned for improved conditions for prison inmates
Robert Peel	One of the conspirators responsible for the Gunpowder Plot
John and Henry Fielding	Controversially executed for the murder of a police officer, causing public outcry
Derek Bentley	Introduced new laws to protect Norman authority in England
Elizabeth Fry	Established the Bow Street Runners
Guy Fawkes	Introduced the Metropolitan Police Act

2 Know the key words

Match each key word below with its definition or description.

Key words	Definitions
Deterrent	A disciplinary measure in which society was expected to work together to bring criminals to justice or face collective punishment
Retribution	The practice of executing someone as punishment for a crime after a proper legal trial
Capital punishment	A physical punishment designed to inflict pain
Collective responsibility	The act of ending a practice or punishment
Penal reform	The process of changing punishments, including conditions in prison
Abolition	The act of making a change to something to improve it
Reform	Something which discourages or is designed to discourage someone from doing something (e.g. committing crime)
Corporal punishment	Punishing a criminal in a way that is equal to the crime that is committed

Part 1 c1000–c1500: Crime and punishment in medieval England

▲ A painting showing William I being crowned as king of England in 1066

Connect and Engage – William I

Born in around 1028, William was the illegitimate son of Duke Robert I of Normandy. William was recognised as the heir to the Duchy of Normandy (a territory, in France, ruled by a duke or duchess) and inherited the role of duke in 1035 when his father died.

From 1047 William dealt with numerous rebellions that threatened to destabilise Normandy and he gained a reputation as a ruthless military commander and leader. At the time, England was made up of Anglo-Saxon earldoms, in which earls controlled the land on behalf of the king, including taking responsibility for law and order.

Under Edward the Confessor, the Godwinson family had become the most powerful earls in England. Harold Godwinson, Earl of Wessex, was particularly popular with the Anglo-Saxons and, after Edward's death, was crowned King of England on 6 January 1066.

Rebellion, rebellion and more rebellion

After his victory over Harold Godwinson at Hastings, William I was crowned King of England in Westminster Abbey on 25 December 1066. This is known as the **Norman Conquest**.

William took the English crown by force and there followed several serious rebellions during the first five years of his reign. These included Exeter, York and East Anglia where there was resistance to Norman rule. He was determined to establish his authority and unite all of England under his control.

The impact of William's rule on crime and punishment

Where necessary, William used brutal methods and force. He used harsh punishments for rebels, which often extended to punishing the whole community by destroying farmland and livestock. It is estimated that around 100,000 people starved to death because of food shortages created by such punishments. Therefore, his reign had a significant impact on crime and punishment.

Under William's rule, the power of the king increased and this included more influence over the law. New definitions of crime were introduced that helped William gain and maintain power. Punishment and law enforcement became more centralised, with less influence from local communities. There was also an increase in the use of harsh punishments, including execution.

> **Connect & Engage**
>
> **Why did challenges to William I's rule influence the law?**
>
> 1. Explain why William faced challenges establishing his authority as king of England.
> 2. Identify the methods William used to overcome these challenges.
> 3. Why do you think William wanted more influence over the law?

1.1 The nature and changing definitions of crime in medieval England

Research & Record

How did definitions of crime change in England during the medieval period?

Copy and complete this table using pages 15–17 to map the change and continuity in definitions of crime in the medieval period.

The nature of crime	Examples from the Anglo-Saxon period	Explanation of change or continuity after the Norman Conquest	Explanation of further change in the later medieval period
Crimes against authority			
Crimes against the person			
Crimes against property			

Before William I

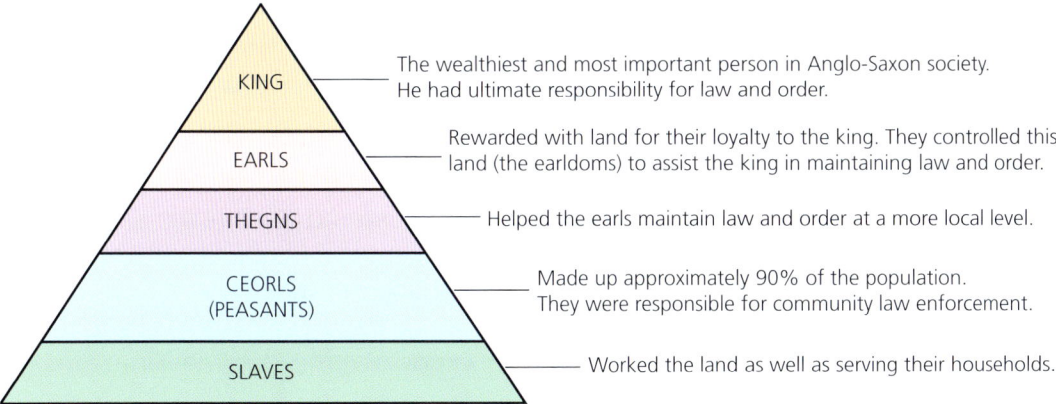

▲ The structure of Anglo-Saxon society, with the king at the top

The Anglo-Saxons had a structured society which defined importance and wealth. This structure influenced their ideas about justice. They believed that:

- the status and position of each group should be clear in the law
- actions that threatened the structure of society were defined as crimes
- earls played an important role in protecting the structure of society by maintaining law and order
- the local community had a responsibility to enforce the law by policing its own behaviour.

Revision Tip

It is easier to learn information when you reduce it into fewer key points. In bullet points, summarise the information on these pages about the role played by each of the following in maintaining law and order in Anglo-Saxon society:

- the king
- earls
- the local community.

15

Definitions of crime in Anglo-Saxon England

Crime in Anglo-Saxon England can be organised into the following types:

Crimes against authority	These crimes were considered the most serious type of crime as they threatened the authority of the king and his nobles and so were a threat to the structure of society. Examples: **treason** (betraying or rebelling against the king) and **betraying your lord**
Crimes against the person	These crimes were actions in which physical force was used against a person and harm caused. Examples: **murder** and **assault**
Crimes against property	These crimes were carried out against personal property, such as a home or possessions. Examples: **theft** and **arson** (setting fire to something)
Some social crimes were actions that were against the law but not viewed disapprovingly by most people in society. The authorities took a very different view of social crimes, classing them as crimes against authority, the person or property, depending on the crime. For example, **poaching** (hunting for food on land you did not own) was a seemingly victimless crime but was actually a crime against authority.	

▲ Definitions of different crimes in Anglo-Saxon England

Changing definitions of crime as a result of the Norman Conquest

Before the Battle of Hastings, Anglo-Saxon systems of law and order were very effective. After the Norman Conquest, William I did not abolish these existing systems. Instead, he amended or added new laws and used harsh punishments to secure his position as king and reinforce his authority.

Murdrum Law

After the Norman Conquest, Anglo-Saxons outnumbered Normans 300 to 1. The Murdrum Law was introduced to protect Normans, who were surrounded by an English population that was unhappy at being conquered. The law stated that if a Norman was murdered by an Anglo-Saxon, the killer would be executed if they were caught. If the killer was not caught, then the **hundred** on which the body was found had to pay a large fine to the king. This was known as the Murdrum Fine.

This law made the murder of a Norman a more serious offence than the murder of an Anglo-Saxon, thus reinforcing Norman authority.

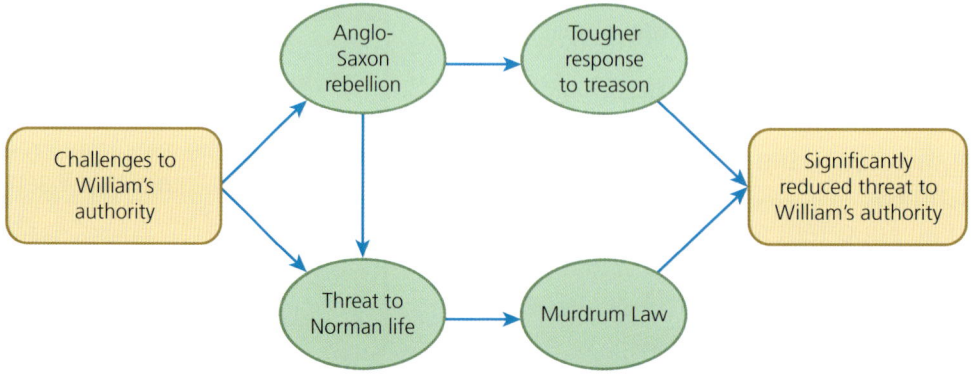

▲ Responses to William I's authority

Forest Laws

Poaching had been illegal under Anglo-Saxon law, but many people had viewed it as a lesser crime. Hunting had been allowed on common land, which was 'free' or 'unowned'. But after the Norman Conquest, William declared some of this land to be royal forest owned by the Crown.

Approximately 30 per cent of England became royal forest, which forced many small communities from the land. The law was unpopular and caused hardship for those who had relied on the natural resources of the land. Only those who could afford to pay to hunt on the land were granted access. Anyone caught poaching was executed.

The law was enforced by foresters who patrolled the land looking for poachers. It was illegal to even carry hunting weapons in the royal forest as it was believed this showed intent to poach. Being caught with a bow and arrow could be punished by the cutting off of fingers, castration (the removal of a male's testicles) or blinding.

This new law made poaching a crime against authority, even though many people viewed it as a social crime (an act that many people do not believe is criminal and therefore are prepared to ignore). Many considered the new **Forest Laws** to be unfair. The punishments for breaking them were deliberately harsh, with the intention to deter people from poaching, and were another method of control through which William could assert his authority.

Crimes in the later medieval period

There were several changes to definitions of crime in the later medieval period. Much like in the Norman period, these changes related to definitions of crime against authority. This shows how maintaining authority was a significant factor throughout the medieval period.

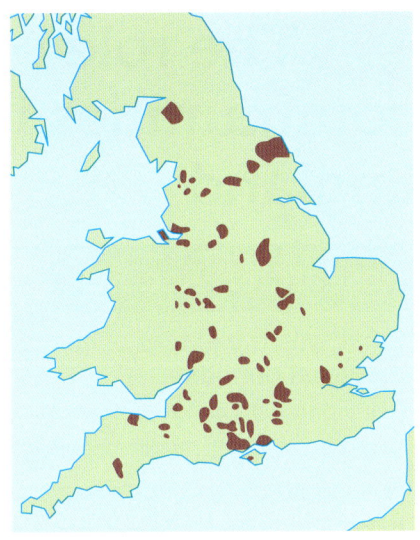

▲ Map of the royal forests in England

> **Revision Tip**
>
> It is important that you know the nature (the type) of crime committed and can make judgements about why these definitions might or might not change over time.
>
> Consider what factors were driving any change. For example, William I's rule had a significant impact on definitions of crime against authority but there was little change in the nature of crime besides this.

Treason	In 1351, the **Treason Act** distinguished between high **treason** (disloyalty to the king) and petty treason (murdering a superior). Both were punishable by death.
Demanding better pay (and working conditions)	In 1348, the Black Death killed approximately one-third of England's population. As a result, there was a shortage of labour and those who were left were in high demand.
	These workers started to demand higher wages for their labour, but, in 1351, the **Statute of Labourers** law made it illegal to ask for higher pay. The law protected the landowners, who were considered above those who worked the land.
Heresy	As head of the Church, the Pope could pass laws to protect the status and position of the Church in society. Some people were openly critical of its wealth and power, but laws passed in 1382 (and again in 1401 and 1414) defined **heresy** – speaking out against God or the Church – as a crime punishable by death.

1.2 The role of the authorities and local communities in law enforcement in medieval England

Research & Record

What was the extent of change to law enforcement in the Anglo-Saxon, Norman and later medieval periods?

Using pages 18–21, complete a copy of this table. Record details of law enforcement in the Anglo-Saxon, Norman and later medieval periods to help form your judgement about change and continuity.

Law enforcement	Anglo-Saxon period	Norman period	Later medieval period
The role of the community			
The role of the authorities			
The role of the Church			

Law enforcement during the Anglo-Saxon period

Before the Norman Conquest in 1066, Anglo-Saxon kings had responsibility for making and enforcing laws. This was known as the king's peace.

The role of the authorities

The king relied on his earls to maintain law and order within their earldoms, but as earldoms covered large areas of land, they were divided into shires to make it easier to manage.

> **SHIRES:** Earldoms were divided into shires. Each shire had a reeve, a local official appointed from within the community who was responsible for bringing suspects to court and making sure punishments were carried out. Over time, the title 'shire reeve' became 'sheriff'. Shire courts were controlled and run by the earl. They met at least twice a year and oversaw trials for serious crimes such as murder.

> **HUNDREDS:** Each shire was divided into hundreds. They were made up of 100 households, which made law and order as well as management of the shire easier. Hundred courts met every month to deal with minor crimes. A jury made up of local men who knew both the accuser and the accused heard evidence from both sides.

> **TITHINGS:** Within each hundred, tithings were formed. A tithing was a group of 10 families from which all men over the age of 12 were responsible for the behaviour of the others. If a member of a tithing committed a crime, the others were responsible for ensuring that person was brought to justice. The whole tithing could be punished, usually with a fine, if they failed to do so.

▲ Law enforcement within the Anglo-Saxon earldoms

The role of the community

There was no police force in Anglo-Saxon England and therefore the community played a large role in law enforcement. They believed that it was the responsibility of the victim and their tithing to find the criminal and bring them to court for justice. This form of **collective responsibility** worked because Anglo-Saxon communities were small and close knit.

▲ A tithing at work

In addition to **tithings**, communities raised the **hue and cry** to track down criminals. When a crime was committed, the victim or witnesses alerted the community with a shout or 'cry'. The community was expected, collectively, to search for the criminal and a person could be fined for failing to participate if they did not have a good reason for not joining the hue and cry.

The role of the Church

The Anglo-Saxons were very religious and the Church played a major role in people's lives.

Trial by ordeal

If a local jury failed to reach a verdict, then **trial by ordeal** was used. In these trials God was the final judge and it was on God's authority that guilt or innocence was decided.

There were four main trials, all of which took place in a church with the priest present. These were trial by hot iron, hot water, sacrament and cold water. Once the ordeal had taken place, the accused returned to the church after three days to hear the verdict. If the accused was found guilty, they would then be punished for their crime.

Trial by hot iron

The accused had to pick up a red-hot iron. The wound was then bandaged. If after three days the wound was not infected, had stayed clean and begun to heal well, this was a sign that God had judged the person to be innocent. Any infection or sign that their hand was not healing was an indication of guilt.

Trial by hot water

The accused had to pick up an object from the bottom of a pot of boiling water. The wound was then bandaged. As with trial by hot iron, if after three days the wound was clean and healing, the accused was deemed innocent. Any infection or sign that their hand was not healing was an indication of guilt.

▲ An ordeal of boiling water from a Sachsenspiegel manuscript (1350–75)

Trial by sacrament

Also referred to as trial by blessed bread, this trial was only used for members of the clergy. The accused priest had to take the blessed bread of communion. Innocence or guilt was determined by how easily the accused could eat the bread as it was believed that if they were guilty, God would cause them to choke.

Trial by cold water

The accused was tied up with rope and lowered into blessed water. Once blessed, the water indicated God's decision of innocence or guilt. If the accused sank, they had been accepted into the water and therefore accepted by God and deemed innocent (they would be removed from the water before they drowned). If they floated, then they had been rejected by the water and therefore by God and were punished accordingly.

Law enforcement during the Norman period

Challenges to William I's authority resulted in changing definitions of crime and harsher punishments. However, he recognised that he had inherited a system of Anglo-Saxon law enforcement that was already effective, so kept many aspects of Anglo-Saxon law enforcement, making additions where necessary.

The role of the community

Collective responsibility was effective because communities were small. As these local communities remained small during the Norman period and were already effective at policing themselves, the Normans kept tithings and the hue and cry. The community also continued to participate in trial by jury.

The role of the authorities

After the Norman Conquest, overall responsibility for law and order remained with the king, just as it had during the Anglo-Saxon period. William used harsher punishment for criminals who threatened his authority (see page 23).

The court system was similar to that used by the Anglo-Saxons:

- Shires were now called 'counties' but shire courts were disbanded. Previously, the royal court had operated only in Westminster. But, in 1166, Henry II ordered royal judges to travel the country in circuit, visiting each county twice a year to hear the most serious criminal cases. This led to the court system becoming more uniform across the country.
- Manor courts were introduced to deal with less serious crimes locally. They were overseen by the lord of the manor and a jury was made-up of the wealthiest villagers.

The role of the Church

The Church saw the biggest changes to law enforcement in the Norman period. Church courts were introduced to deal with moral crimes such as adultery. They were only for churchmen, but since a range of people besides priests had roles in the Church, that did not stop ordinary people claiming '**benefit of clergy**' in order to use them because the Church courts had a reputation for leniency, with less harsh punishments (see page 19).

Tension between Norman monarchs and the Church increased throughout the period, with monarchs becoming increasingly concerned that not everyone was subject to the authority of the same courts. However, the Normans continued to allow God to decide innocence or guilt when an outcome could not be reached in court. They introduced a new trial known as trial by combat, in which the accused and their accuser would fight each other, often to the death. It was believed that God would influence the outcome of the battle to indicate who was guilty and who was innocent.

▲ A drawing from the 1200s showing trial by combat

Law enforcement during the later medieval period

By the later medieval period changes to law enforcement were necessary. Towns were growing, especially London, and their increased populations provided more opportunities for crime. As a result, law enforcement became more centralised, with more involvement from the authorities. Previously popular methods of community policing were no longer as effective within these larger communities. But there was some continuity from the Norman period.

- The hue and cry remained, with locals expected to look out for people committing crime within their communities.
- Local juries were still used to deal with less serious crimes in manor courts.
- The royal court continued to deal with serious crimes.

There were, however, some important changes.

Parish constables

Shire reeves from the Anglo-Saxon period became 'sheriffs'. In the 1200s sheriffs would organise a posse (a group of local men) to help find a suspected criminal if they had not been found by the hue and cry. In 1285 the Statute of Winchester, the legislation that regulated what we now refer to as policing, stated that it was the responsibility of everyone to apprehend criminals and keep the peace, and the idea of a 'watch' of watchmen was first introduced. The law led to the introduction of **parish constables** to replace sheriffs. They were respected members of the local community who volunteered for the unpaid position for the duration of a year. They were expected to keep the peace in their spare time by keeping a lookout for crime, arresting criminals and leading the hue and cry.

The royal court

Previously, the royal court, had operated just in Westminster. But, in 1166, Henry II ordered royal judges to travel the country in circuit, visiting each county twice a year to hear the most serious criminal cases. This circuit came to be known as the assizes, after the Assize of Clarendon – the name given to the law introduced by Henry II that transformed English law. The law increased the role of the king in legal matters and meant that the system was becoming more uniform across the country.

Justices of the peace

During the twelfth century the king appointed knights to maintain law and order in more unruly areas of the country. They became known as keepers of the peace. In 1327, the role changed to become **justices of the peace** (JPs), and was introduced to every area of the country. Their job was to uphold the king's peace. JPs were usually members of the gentry. The role was unpaid, but they had the power to arrest criminals. They met four times a year to enforce the law. These became known as quarter sessions, becoming the main courts for serious crimes that did not carry the death penalty and therefore were not tried by the royal courts.

1.3 The nature of punishment in medieval England

Research & Record

To what extent did the nature of punishment change throughout the medieval period?
Use pages 22 and 23 to complete a copy of this table. Record examples of punishment throughout the period to show how different methods continued or changed over time.

	Anglo-Saxon period	Norman period	Later medieval period
Capital punishment			
Corporal punishment			
Compensation			
Humiliation			

Aims and methods of punishment in medieval England

Throughout the medieval period, punishment served two main aims:

- **deterrence** – to put off others from committing crime
- **retribution** – to gain revenge by delivering justice for those affected by the crime.

There were different methods for achieving deterrence and retribution. These varied slightly across the Anglo-Saxon, Norman and later medieval periods, but they shared the principle that the more severe the crime, the more severe the punishment.

Capital punishment

The most severe form of retribution was **capital punishment** in which the criminal paid with their life. Executions were carried out by hanging or beheading in public. This was thought to provide the ultimate deterrent.

Corporal punishment

Corporal punishment is a punishment that inflicts pain on the body. It often involved branding (burning a letter or a mark onto the body with a hot iron rod), whipping or maiming the criminal by cutting off a body part. For example, a thief might have a hand chopped off, reducing their ability to commit the crime again and leaving them with a visible **deterrent** to other potential thieves.

Compensation

A **fine** could be given as punishment so that a criminal paid money to the king or to the victim or victim's family to repay them for their losses. Failure to pay the fine, even if the criminal did not have enough money, resulted in a more serious punishment.

Humiliation

Punishment such as the stocks and pillory aimed to humiliate the criminal and shame them into not committing crime again in the future. Shaming the wrongdoer in public also served as a warning to the whole community.

Punishment in Anglo-Saxon England

The most serious criminals, such as those who had committed treason, were punished by hanging or beheading. Capital punishment was thought to be an important part of deterring those who may commit crimes that would undermine the social hierarchy.

The Anglo-Saxons also used compensation, corporal punishment and humiliation as forms of punishment:

- A system of fines known as '**Wergild**' was introduced to compensate the victims of crime or their families using money. The amount of Wergild depended on the type of crime and the social status of the victim. Murder carried a higher price than physical injury, and the price for a noble victim was higher than that for a peasant. In cases of physical injury, each body part had its own price. Wergild continued throughout the Anglo-Saxon period, but increasingly capital punishment became the preferred punishment for murder.
- Corporal punishment was used for a range of crimes against the person or property, including assault and theft. This could include removing a body part that was necessary to commit the crime, called maiming.
- Humiliation was used for lesser crimes such as public disorder and drunkenness. The stocks and pillory (wooden structures used to secure the criminals' feet or hands and neck) made criminals a public spectacle as they were deliberately placed in the centre of the village. Members of the community might shout abuse or throw things at them. Criminals were left for days through all weathers.

▲ Illustration of medieval people in the stocks

Changes to punishment after the Norman Conquest

William I ended the Wergild. Instead, he ordered fines to be paid directly to the king's officials. In addition, fines were introduced as part of the new Murdrum Law.

However, there was also continuity between the two periods. Deterrence and retribution continued to be the main aims of punishment. The Normans used capital punishment for serious crimes and re-offenders; corporal punishment to punish people who broke the new Forest Laws (see page 17); and fines, the stocks and pillory for petty crimes.

There was a huge increase in the number of executions and corporal punishments as William wanted to enforce his authority. In particular, William considered the many Anglo-Saxon rebellions against Norman rule to be acts of treason. He dealt with them particularly harshly, punishing those actively involved in rebelling but also others in their communities. The most serious rebellion occurred in 1069 in the north of England. William's response became known as the Harrying of the North. William's army killed hundreds of people and destroyed their crops and livestock, which meant that many more people starved. His harsh actions were meant to be a deterrent, which would stop others from rebelling.

There was little further change to punishment in the later medieval period. However, in the fourteenth century a new punishment was introduced for high treason. Following the 1351 Treason Act, a man convicted of plotting to kill or betray the king was sentenced to be hanged, drawn and quartered. Women convicted of high treason were to be burned at the stake.

1.4 Case study: The influence of the Church on crime and punishment in the early thirteenth century

> ### Research & Record
>
> **How did the influence of the Church on crime and punishment change during the later medieval period?**
>
> Use the case studies and information boxes on these two pages to gather examples under these two headings.
>
> **The Church**
> - The Church offered sanctuary to criminals.
> -
>
> **The authorities**
> - Monarchs wanted to limit the power of church courts.
> -

The influence of the Church on crime and punishment changed during the later medieval period, mostly because monarchs wanted more control over the way the law was enforced.

Throughout the later medieval period, law enforcement underwent some big changes. As the population increased and towns and cities grew, the community policing methods of the Anglo-Saxons and the Normans came under more strain. As a result, more centralised methods were introduced, bringing law enforcement under the control of officials appointed by the king. The role of local communities was still important, but these changes allowed the authorities to oversee at both a national and a local level.

Royal courts and justices of the peace had made the system fairer and more efficient. However, by the thirteenth century, monarchs were beginning to express their concern about the Church's role in law enforcement and the handing out of more lenient punishments through Church courts. In response, the Church became concerned that monarchs wanted to reduce their influence by limiting the power of the Church courts.

The end of trial by ordeal

In deciding who was guilty or innocent, trial by ordeal demonstrated the power of God and the Church. However, in 1215, Pope Innocent III forbade clergymen from organising ordeals. The Pope disagreed with the use of trial by ordeal because it was unreliable. It was possible for innocent people to be found guilty and vice versa. Without the priests to organise the trials, trial by ordeal soon ended. Ordeals were replaced with trial by jury.

Benefit of clergy

Despite the end of trial by ordeal, the Church continued to influence crime and punishment through Church courts. The term 'benefit of clergy' describes the process of clergymen being tried at a Church court rather than in a royal court. It was considered a 'benefit' because Church courts gave less harsh punishments than other courts and capital punishment was never used.

Officially, Church courts were only for clergy members who had committed moral crimes, such as failure to attend church or drunkenness. To gain access to church courts, the accused had to prove that they were a clergyman. This involved reading a passage from the Bible, which it was believed only clergymen could do because most other people could not read. Some people tried to memorise a Bible passage in order to pass as members of the clergy. This gained the nickname 'the neck verse' because it could save your neck from the noose.

The Church courts' lenient attitude towards punishment caused conflict with some monarchs. In the late twelfth century, Henry II unsuccessfully tried to limit the power of the Church courts. He wanted more control over law enforcement and punishment and believed Church courts challenged his authority. However, Church courts continued to operate well into the seventeenth century.

Sanctuary

Throughout the medieval period criminals could claim **sanctuary** in a church if they were able to get there before capture. Protection from the Church lasted for 40 days and nobody, including the sheriff, had the power to arrest the person during this time. During the 40-day period the suspect had to decide whether they would face trial or leave the country.

▲ The sanctuary knocker at Durham Cathedral. The criminal would use the knocker to be let in. A church bell would be rung to alert people that someone had claimed sanctuary

Revision Tip

Practise applying your knowledge

It is important that you regularly practise retrieving and using your knowledge.

Look at the example paragraph below. It explains how the Church influenced attitudes in one aspect of crime and punishment during the period. Note how the highlighted connective 'this meant that' starts a sentence that helps to develop the answer – proving that this factor played an important role.

1 Complete this first paragraph to explain how the Church's influence changed in the thirteenth century.
2 Write a second paragraph to explain another way in which the Church influenced medieval crime and punishment. For example, you could explore how the Church took a more lenient approach to punishment and why this led to conflict with the authorities in the later medieval period.

> One way in which the Church influenced crime and punishment throughout the medieval period was the use of trial by ordeal. The Anglo-Saxons subjected the accused to ordeal by cold water, hot water, hot iron or consecrated bread. This meant that people at the time believed God had the final say in whether the accused was innocent or guilty. If found guilty, the criminal was sentenced and punished. The Normans continued the practice and introduced trial by combat. However, in 1215 the Pope ordered that priests should stop organising trials by ordeal. As a result …

1.5 Medieval period review

Review 1

Continuity and change

1. The period summary chart below summarises the medieval period. Study it carefully, then create a blank copy (with only the themes listed on the left-hand side) and try to reproduce all the information from memory alone. Use a whole page of A4 paper with three rows – one per theme. This is a challenge but worth the effort because it will reveal what you are able to remember easily and what you are finding harder to recall.
2. Once you have done the best you can, review your attempt against the period summary chart below. Fill in any gaps using a different coloured pen. This will remind you what you are struggling to remember.

Period summary c1000–c1500		
Theme	**Evidence of continuity**	**Evidence of change**
Definitions of crime	• Throughout the period crimes against authority were defined as the most serious of crimes. This reflected the hierarchical structure of society in the medieval period.	• The Norman Conquest in 1066 influenced attitudes towards crimes against authority. • Changing definitions such as the Murdrum Law were introduced to protect Norman authority. • The Forest Laws made poaching a crime against authority, although many people continued to view it as a social crime. • In the later medieval period, the new definition of treason to include high treason (disloyalty to the king) demonstrated the individual importance of the monarch.
Enforcing the law	• Both Anglo-Saxon and Norman societies relied heavily upon local communities to enforce the law through tithings and the hue and cry. • In addition, both the authorities and the Church played a role in enforcing the law, through a system of official courts and trial by ordeal. • Across the whole medieval period, the king was responsible for law and order. • The influence of the Church also continued, despite attempts by monarchs to reduce it.	• The Normans introduced trial by combat as a new ordeal. • They also introduced Church courts to deal with moral crimes, reflecting the importance of the Church during this period. • In the later medieval period, law enforcement became more centralised with the introduction of JPs and parish constables, which meant the role of the local communities was overseen by royal officials. • Trial by ordeal ended in 1215.

Theme	Evidence of continuity	Evidence of change
Punishment: the emphasis on deterrence and retribution	• In the absence of an official police force, deterrence and retribution were an important part of enforcing the law (crime prevention). • Throughout the period, severe punishments aimed to deter potential criminals from committing crime. • Retribution reflected attitudes to crime, with the harshest of punishments used for crimes against authority.	• The Normans ended the Anglo-Saxon practice of Wergild; instead, punishment was administered by the authorities and fines were paid directly to the king's officials. This demonstrated the importance of Norman authority. • There were also harsher punishments for rebellion, which often extended to the wider community and not just the instigators. • In the later medieval period, men found guilty of high treason were sentenced to be hanged, drawn and quartered.

Review 2

What factors influenced crime and punishment in the years c1000 to c1500?

It is important to understand the factors that are influencing and driving change in each time period that you study. These factors are:
- attitudes in society
- the role of individuals and institutions, such as the Church and government/authorities
- science and technology.

During the medieval period, developments in science and technology had little impact on crime and punishment, but there is lots of evidence to support the roles played by society, individuals, government/authority and the Church during this period.

Using the information throughout Part 1, complete a copy of this table. Include specific names, dates or events to show what was influencing change and continuity across the medieval period.

Factor	How it influenced change	How it influenced continuity
Individuals	William I was driven by his need to assert authority. This resulted in changes to definitions of crime against authority with the introduction of the Murdrum Law and the Forest Laws.	William I inherited an effective system of Anglo-Saxon law enforcement. Therefore, the Normans continued to rely upon local communities to enforce the law through a system of tithings and the hue and cry.
Institutions: the Church		
Institutions: government/ authority		
Attitudes in society		

1.6 Medieval period exam practice

Revision Tip

Regularly revisit content to make sure it sticks

You have just completed the first part of the course and it may be tempting to move quickly on to Part 2. However, it is important to build in regular revision activities as you progress through your GCSE course.

How do you stop yourself forgetting? The key is to regularly revisit information you have covered. The revision challenges below revisit material from this part of the course.

Apply ▶ Recall Challenges

1 Know the definitions and nature of crime in the medieval period

Draw the graphics onto an A4 piece of paper, creating three columns or boxes that you can add detail to. Each graphic represents a definition of crime. Using the prompts below, add specific detail to each box.

a What type of crime does each graphic represent?

b For each type of crime, list as many specific examples as you can think of.

c Now, using a different coloured pen, add the types of punishment that were used to punish each type of crime.

2 Know the key words

Make an A4 copy of this bingo card. You will need plenty of space to write in each box.

Key word bingo		
Sanctuary	Benefit of clergy	Church courts
Murdrum	Justice of the peace	Treason
Maiming	Capital punishment	Stocks & pillory

a For each key word or phrase, write a definition from memory. Then check your definition against the information in this chapter and in the glossary on pages 134–35.

b For each word in the top row, explain how it was linked to the influence of the Church.

c For each word in the middle row, explain how it was linked to the role of authority.

d For each word in the bottom row, explain how it provided deterrence.

Exam Tip

Use specific knowledge

You can improve your exam answers by including relevant facts to support your arguments. For example, when answering the question on page 29:

- Do not simply describe methods of law enforcement such as the tithing, explain how this links to the role of the community and its significance to law enforcement at the time.
- Explain how justices of the peace were significant to law enforcement in the later medieval period. Use this point to develop a counter-argument that shows the importance of the role of the authorities.

Exam Tip

Making a judgement (question 5/6)

When answering question 5 or 6, you must make a judgement about how far you agree with the statement. The easiest way to do this is to write a conclusion at the end of your answer. The best answers will have their overall judgement running throughout the answer. For example, when answering the question on page 29:

- Decide whether you agree or disagree that the role of the local community was the most important factor in medieval law enforcement and begin your paragraph with *'In conclusion, the statement can be disagreed with …'*
- Go on to explain why you have reached this judgement by saying that there were other important factors such as the role of the authorities and the Church.

Exam Tip

Question 5/6: Judgement question

Your exam will have a question that asks for you to make a judgement about how far you agree with a statement about causation, consequence, change, continuity or significance. Think before you write using the 3Ds: **decode**, **decide** and **develop**.

Decode the question (work out the focus of the question). Staying focused on the question is crucial. Including information that is not relevant or writing about the wrong topic wastes time and gains no marks. Here's how to 'decode' a question.

What are the command words?
The question asks, 'How far do you agree?' You need to agree and disagree with the statement before reaching a judgement.

What is the content focus?
Focus on the role of the community in law enforcement. Weigh this against the other factors that influenced law enforcement in medieval England, such as the authorities and the Church. You need to include at least three aspects of knowledge throughout your answer.

> 'The role of local communities was the most important factor in law enforcement in the years c1000–c1500.'
>
> How far do you agree? Explain your answer. (16 marks)
>
> You may use the following in your answer:
> - tithings
> - trial by ordeal.
>
> You **must** also use information of your own.

What is the conceptual focus?
The historical concept is significance. Describing different methods of law enforcement is not enough to get the higher-level marks. Focus on explaining why you agree and disagree that the local community was the most important factor in medieval law enforcement, then support with examples from your knowledge.

How many marks are available?
'16 marks' indicates you should spend about 30 minutes on the question. You should try to write at least three paragraphs: at least one paragraph that agrees with the statement, at least one that disagrees and a conclusion.

There are also 4 marks for SPaG, that means your spelling, punctuation and grammar. Check that you have spelled key terms, used capital letters, commas, full stops and paragraphs correctly.

Decide how to organise your answer into paragraphs. You do not have the time to tell the story of medieval law enforcement. The focus is on the importance of the role of local communities within law enforcement in this period. Decide the main arguments you want to explain and then organise these reasons into three paragraphs. One possible approach is:

- Paragraph 1: Agree with the statement – explain how the role of local communities, in particular the use of tithings, was important to medieval law enforcement.
- Paragraph 2: Agree with the statement – explain that there were other important community-based methods of law enforcement, such as the hue and cry.
- Paragraph 3: Disagree with the statement – explain how religious ideas, such as the use of trial by ordeal, also influenced law enforcement.
- Paragraph 4: End with a conclusion – decide whether you agree or disagree with the statement overall and explain why.

Develop your answer in relation to the question.
- Make sure you explain and support the points you make. Do not simply state that the role of local communities was important to medieval law enforcement – explain how and give specific examples.
- Do not simply state that other factors influenced medieval law enforcement. Explain these factors and explain that they were not linked to local communities.

Part 2 c1500–c1700: Crime and punishment in early modern England

Connect and Engage – Guy Fawkes

Guy Fawkes was born in 1570 near York, during a time of religious instability in England. Guy's father passed away when he was eight years old and the family converted to Catholicism from the Church of England after his mother remarried into a Catholic family.

In 1591 Fawkes travelled to Europe to fight in the Eighty Years War for Catholic Spain. This put him at odds with an English population who were mostly Protestant and saw Spain as an enemy after the attempted invasion of England led by the Spanish Armada in 1588.

When he returned, Fawkes became involved with a small group of Catholic Englishmen led by Robert Catesby. They planned to assassinate England's Protestant king, James I in what would become known as the Gunpowder Plot (see pages 42–43).

▲ Guy Fawkes, one of the Gunpowder Plotters

The plot to kill the King was unsuccessful and the Gunpowder Plotters were arrested. Fawkes, who had endured days of torture after his arrest on 4 November 1605, had sealed his fate and that of his fellow Gunpowder Plotters with two signed confessions on 8 and 9 November. The confessions revealed the names of the plotters and their plans to murder James I and his heir by blowing up the Houses of Parliament with gunpowder.

On 31 January 1606 a crowd gathered in Old Palace Yard, just outside Westminster Hall in London, where four days previously eight men had been found guilty of high treason and sentenced to death. The crowd had come to witness the execution of Guy Fawkes and three of his co-conspirators.

The men were drawn on wooden panels against the ground behind horses through the streets of London to the execution site. They were hanged until close to death, then pulled down, cut open and some body parts were removed. The heads and other body parts of Fawkes and his fellow conspirators were set on spikes around London to serve as a warning to others.

Connect & Engage

Use the information on this page to answer these questions:

1. What crime was Guy Fawkes found guilty of? Use your prior knowledge to explain why this was a serious crime.
2. Explain why religion is an important factor in the story of the Gunpowder Plot.
3. Why do you think Guy Fawkes and his fellow conspirators were punished so severely?

2.1 Change and continuity in definitions of crime in early modern England

There was much continuity between the medieval and early modern periods. Crimes against the person, such as murder, and crimes against property, such as theft, were handled as they had been in the later medieval period.

There was also some continuity for crimes against authority. Treason had always been considered the most serious crime which had always triggered a severe response from the authorities.

However, while attitudes to treason in the medieval period were driven mostly by threats to power and the structured hierarchy of society, by the early modern period a new factor was influencing attitudes to crimes against authority: religious turmoil and paranoia.

The impact of religion on definitions of crime

At the start of the sixteenth century, England was a Catholic country but this changed in 1534 when King Henry VIII split from the Catholic Church and made himself head of the Church in England instead of the Pope. This event is known as the English Reformation. This was not the only time that the official religion of England changed in early modern England (see below):

The impact on heresy and treason

Heresy, the crime of holding religious views which were banned, was not a new crime. However, as the official religion kept changing in the sixteenth century, people were at greater risk of breaking the law because of their religious beliefs. People whose faith did not align with that of the monarch were heretics. While heretics in the medieval period had usually been punished with fines, although could receive a capital sentence, in the early modern period, more people accused of heresy were found guilty and sentenced to death.

The Reformation also had an impact on treason as monarchs faced plots to overthrow them and replace them with a monarch of the opposite religion. Now that the monarch was head of the Church of England, acts of heresy could also be viewed as acts of high treason.

The impact of religion on heresy and treason was most noticeable during the years 1534–1603 while new churches and ways of worship were being established. After this period there was more religious stability. However, religion continued to affect attitudes to crime and definitions of new crime well into the seventeenth century.

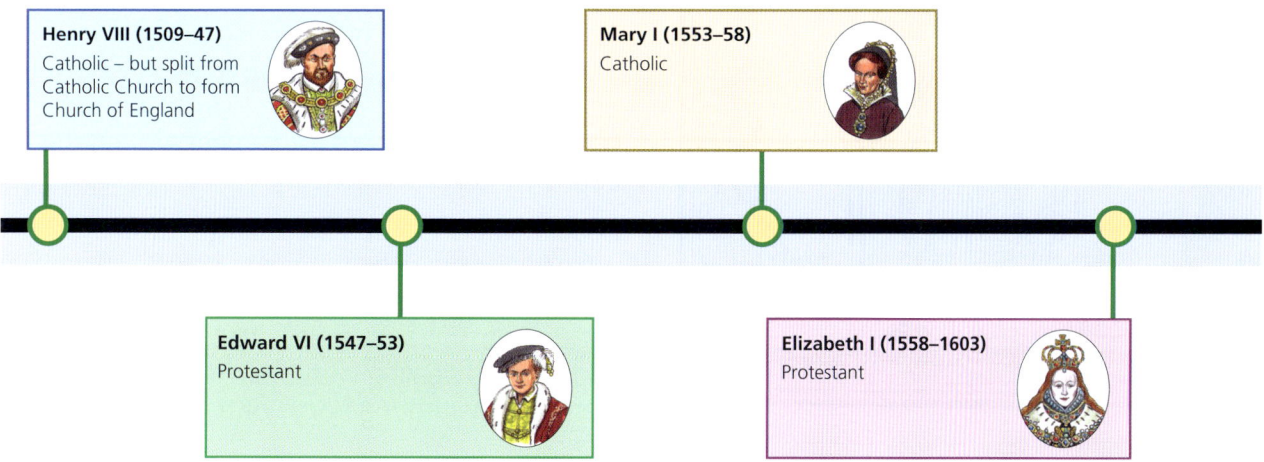

▲ How the official religion of England changed from the reign of Henry VIII to the reign of his daughter Elizabeth I

New definitions of crime c1500–c1700

As well as changing definitions of existing crimes, religion also influenced definitions of new crimes in the early modern period. In addition, social and economic changes throughout the period, individuals, changes in the attitudes of society and scientific understanding also influenced definitions of crime.

Research & Record

Which factors influenced new definitions of crime in the early modern period?

Use pages 32–36 to complete a copy of this table. Write a description of each new crime. Then, using the list of factors below, make a judgement about which factor, or factors, influenced each definition of a new crime. Provide a justification for your choice.

- Authorities
- Individuals
- The Church
- Science
- Attitudes in society

New crimes	The nature of the crime (description)	Factor(s) influencing the crime
Vagabondage		
Witchcraft		
Smuggling		
Poaching		

▲ A contemporary woodcut showing a seventeenth-century vagrant traveller holding a brace of poached rabbits

Vagabondage

By the beginning of the sixteenth century, England was experiencing an increase in population. This led to a growth in demand for food and jobs, which in turn led to higher rates of unemployment and food shortages. As a result, people often left their home villages in search of work, creating more movement around the country than previously.

People who were homeless and unemployed were known as vagabonds or vagrants. Despite poverty being a major factor in the increase in vagabonds, the authorities still took a hostile approach to dealing with them. **Vagabondage** – wandering without a home or a job – became a crime.

Why was there concern about vagabonds?

There were various reasons that people were concerned about vagabonds.

- The increase in homelessness and unemployment sparked fears that vagabonds could rebel against the authorities.
- Others worried that vagabonds would commit other crimes such as theft, assault or even murder to get money.
- The increased movement of people searching for work concerned the wealthier classes, who worried that their property and wealth could be threatened by those experiencing hardship.
- The authorities and wealthier classes harshly believed vagabonds to be capable of work, but lazy and therefore undeserving of help. The 'deserving poor' were those who had fallen upon hardship through no fault of their own and the wealthy already paid poor rates to their local parish to support them.

How did the authorities deal with vagabonds?

The authorities responded to these fears by passing several laws to deal with vagrancy.

1536 Act for Punishment of Vagabonds and Beggars

Passed by Henry VIII, the law stated that vagabonds be set to work after they had been punished. They were publicly whipped through the streets for a first offence but could be maimed or even executed if caught for a second or third time.

1547 Vagrancy Act

Vagabonds who were capable of work were to be branded with the letter V (burned into their flesh with a hot metal rod) and sold into slavery for a period of two years. This Act was later repealed as it was too harsh.

1597 Act for the Relief of the Poor

Elizabeth I passed a law in which the poor were categorised as deserving or undeserving. Overseers were appointed within each parish and they provided relief to the deserving poor: the aged, sick and infant poor. Those who were able bodied were given work. All previous laws in which vagrants received corporal punishment were removed.

1601 Poor Law

This law was a refinement of the 1597 Act for the Relief of the Poor. It established workhouses and hospitals for the relief of the deserving poor and those capable of work. Houses of correction could be used for those deemed to be lazy.

Witchcraft

Belief in witches was not new to the early modern period. A belief in magic had long been widely accepted by society as scientific understanding had not developed sufficiently to explain good or bad fortune. People believed that witches made a pact with the devil in exchange for magical powers, which included the ability to harm crops, animals and people, or even to cause death.

Witchcraft had been a crime in the medieval period, but cases of witchcraft were dealt with by church courts, meaning convicted witches did not face the death penalty. However, fears of witchcraft increased dramatically throughout the early modern period and many more people were accused of being witches. The accused would be forced to take the swimming test (trial by cold water). This was not a punishment; it was a way to test guilt. If the 'witch' floated, they were a witch and were punished. Several new laws made the punishment for witchcraft harsher. The usual punishment was hanging. Although some men were accused and found guilty of witchcraft, the vast majority of those accused were women.

1541 Witchcraft Act

Henry VIII was the first monarch to make significant changes to the way in which witchcraft accusations were dealt with. His law defined harmful or destructive acts of witchcraft as a capital offence, meaning that those convicted of such acts would face the death penalty. Harmless acts of witchcraft such as healing the sick were not considered criminal. The law was repealed by his son Edward VI in 1547.

1562 Act Against Conjurations, Enchantments and Witchcrafts

In 1562, Elizabeth I introduced new laws which defined 'minor witchcraft' and 'major witchcraft'. Minor witchcraft, which included the use of magic and charms, could be punished with the stocks. Major witchcraft such as causing death became a capital offence punished by the death penalty.

1603 Act Against Conjuration, Witchcraft, and dealing with evil and wicked Spirits

In 1603, James I's law kept Elizabeth I's distinction between major and minor cases of witchcraft but put more emphasis on the relationship between the witch and the devil. Trying to raise the spirits of the dead or invoking evil spirits were also punished by death.

Why did the number of witchcraft accusations increase in the early modern period?

New laws were introduced to deal with witchcraft and the number of prosecutions for witchcraft increased because the attitudes of the authorities and wider society changed during this period. This happened for several reasons.

Religion

Religion and the Church were still an important part of daily life and helped to shape attitudes towards witchcraft. After Henry VIII broke away from the Catholic Church there was a period of religious upheaval in which paranoia and fear increased. This fear led to an increase in witch trials as people grew more suspicious of those within their communities who did not fit in.

Daemonologie

In 1597, James VI of Scotland published a book called *Daemonologie*. James was both fascinated and fearful of witches because he believed he had personal experience of them. Witches, he said, had claimed responsibility for trying to drown his new wife by sinking her ship on her voyage from Denmark to Scotland. The book made a clear link between witches and the devil and it encouraged people to seek out witches, offering instruction on how to run witch trials. James argued that witchcraft was a crime not only against the king but against God and he brought these views to England in 1603 when he was crowned James I.

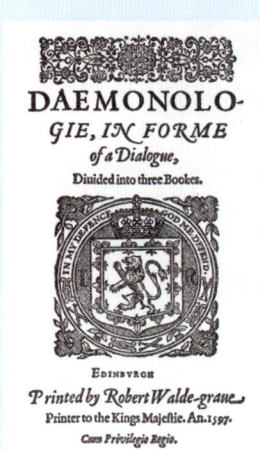

Social upheaval

From 1642 until 1651, England experienced civil war. There was huge disruption and uncertainty, which left families divided, by their loyalties to either king or parliament, or by the war itself as men left the family home to fight. The war created an atmosphere of fear in which witch accusations could thrive.

Economic hardship

The English civil wars left more women at home alone at a time when most relied on the income of their husbands. More women needed to support themselves and some turned to selling herbal remedies to earn money. In addition, a cold spell of weather referred to by historians as a 'mini-ice age' led to an increase in crop failure and food shortages. Without scientific knowledge able to explain this, witches were assumed to be the cause.

Revision Tip

As you learn about crime and punishment in Britain c1000 to the present day, it is important to look for examples of change and continuity in:
- definitions and the nature of crime
- approaches to punishment and law enforcement.

For the early modern period, write notes under these headings, giving examples of change and continuity for the period. You could organise this information in a table.

Smuggling

During the sixteenth and seventeenth centuries explorers discovered more of the Americas. As a result, England began to build up an empire based on overseas trade and started to import some new goods such as tea, spices, tobacco and alcohol. These new goods were considered luxury items and therefore the government introduced import duties on them, a tax payable on imported goods.

Smuggling is the act of moving something in or out of a country illegally. This might be because the product itself is illegal or, more commonly, it is where those bringing them into the country have not paid the import duties to the government for them. During the sixteenth and seventeenth centuries there was a rise in smuggling as more goods were being imported and people tried to avoid paying heavy tax on these imported items. Smugglers mostly operated at night when their boats were difficult to see.

To many, smuggling was a social crime and not a serious one because people thought it was victimless. The victim of the crime was the government, which lost the taxation money on the goods. There were plenty of people who were willing to buy from smugglers because they sold goods for a cheaper price.

▲ A reconstruction drawing of smugglers landing a cargo boat on a remote beach to avoid paying taxes

Poaching

During the early modern period a process known as enclosure was introduced to manage land and farming. Areas of common land that had been accessible to the public were fenced off for private use, either for sheep grazing or farming or for landlords to hunt and fish privately. This had a huge impact on the rural poor who had relied upon the common land for hunting, wild foods and firewood.

Similar to William I's Forest Laws (see page 17), enclosure led to an increase in prosecutions for poaching as many poor people continued to hunt or fish where they had always done but these were now enclosed areas. In 1671 the Game Act allowed aristocrats and gentlemen to hunt, but made this illegal for the lower classes, and anyone who was caught poaching could receive the death penalty. Despite the new law, the authorities struggled to stamp out poaching. The upper classes considered poachers to be trespassers and therefore a threat to their land. But there was a lot of sympathy for poachers from people who were not wealthy and, as with smuggling, many viewed it as a social crime. In fact, the new law led to an increase in gangs who began to poach in groups, knowing that this would make it more difficult for the authorities to catch them, which created a new problem for the authorities to deal with.

Apply ▶ Exam Practice

Question 3 style

Use the Exam Tip to help you answer these comparing time periods questions:

A Explain one way in which attitudes towards poaching in the period c1000 to c1500 were similar to attitudes towards poaching in the period c1500 to c1700. **(4 marks)**

B Explain one way in which the definition of crimes against authority in the period c1000 to c1500 was similar to the definition of crime against authority in the period c1500 to c1700. **(4 marks)**

Exam Tip

Comparing time periods (Question 3)

Use the steps below to help you answer the questions in the Exam Practice box above.

Step 1: Identify the content focus of the question. Both questions compare one feature (attitudes towards poaching and definitions of crime against authority) in two different time periods.

Step 2: Identify the conceptual focus of the question. Both questions ask for similarities between the periods. Focus on similarity. Do not write about differences.

Step 3: Write. You will have about 6 minutes to answer this type of 4-mark question. Aim for four or five sentences. Identify a similarity and develop this with explanation. Include an example from both periods.

See the possible answer to the first question. Choose some different examples in your answer to this question.

Possible answer to 3A

During the period c1000 to c1500 many people saw poaching as a social crime. William I introduced the Forest Laws in which 30 per cent of England became royal forest owned by the Crown. This caused hardship for those who relied on the land for hunting and so there was a lot of public sympathy for poachers but it was actually a crime against authority. Attitudes to poaching in the period c1500 to c1700 were similar because of enclosure which limited the use of common land for hunting. The public continued to be sympathetic to poachers and often turned a blind eye to poaching but it remained a crime against authority.

A similarity in public attitudes towards poaching in both periods has been identified – many people believed it to be a victimless social crime, but it was a crime against authority.

This point is supported with an example from each time period.

Revision Tip

You will learn about the nature of crime in Britain from c1000 to the present day. Look for change and continuity in:
- attitudes to crimes against the person, property and authority
- the factors that influence these attitudes, such as religion, science and individuals.

2.2 The role of the authorities and local communities in law enforcement c1500–c1700

Research & Record

Who was responsible for enforcing the law in the years c1500 to c1700?

Use pages 38 and 39 to complete this table. Record examples of who was responsible for law enforcement and how this was done.

The role of the authorities	The role of local communities

Continuity in law enforcement

Law enforcement in early modern England was similar to that of the medieval period in a number of ways:

- The local community was still expected to join the hue and cry to chase down suspected criminals and bring them to justice.
- Local men took on the role of parish constable. They were appointed by the parish, with the role unpaid and organised locally rather than centralised by the authorities. Parish constables were still expected to lead the hue and cry.
- Manor courts continued to deal with local cases of minor crime. Verdicts were decided by a local jury.
- The royal court at Westminster and the assizes circuit of royal judges continued to operate.
- The role of the justice of the peace continued into the early modern period.

Changes in law enforcement

The role of the parish constable and town watchman

During the early modern period England's population steadily increased and towns and cities grew rapidly. London became one of the largest cities in Europe and England's increasing prosperity led to increased temptation for thieves. Community law enforcement was less effective in large towns where people were less likely to know each other, and this led to change in the traditional role of constable.

Parish constables continued to operate in smaller communities. But in the larger towns and cities additional law enforcement was needed. **Town watchmen**, like parish constables, were expected to keep watch for crime and arrest suspected criminals, including vagabonds. Every male householder was expected to take their turn on the night watch. Watchmen patrolled the streets at night with a lantern, bell and weapon. This was intended to deter criminals, but the role was

▲ A drawing of a town watchman from around 1600

unpaid until 1663, meaning that some watchmen did not take the role seriously and were therefore ineffective. In 1663, Charles II established a force of paid watchmen to patrol the streets of towns and cities. They became known as Charlies, but there is little evidence the pay made them more effective or respected by their communities.

The role of justices of the peace

As the population grew and the number of crimes and court cases increased, the role of the JP expanded. A JP had the power to deal with more cases of minor crime independently or in pairs, rather than at quarter sessions. They still met four times a year with other JPs in quarter sessions, where they were able to deal with more serious crimes and had the power to pass a sentence of death. In addition, they oversaw parish constables and town watchmen.

The role of the courts

Both JPs and the assizes experienced an increase in work because of an increasing number of charges for theft and serious crimes. In addition, the passing of the Habeas Corpus Act in 1679 prevented the authorities from holding a suspected criminal in prison indefinitely without charging them with a crime. They had to appear in court within a reasonable timeframe or be released.

The role of the Church

The role of the Church in law enforcement had become a matter of concern in the later medieval period, and monarchs in the early modern period continued to challenge its power and authority with some limited success. In the early modern period, Church courts were eventually phased out.

In 1512, Henry VIII restricted the power of the Church by removing benefit of clergy for serious crimes such as murder, meaning even clergymen had to be tried in secular (non-religious) courts.

In 1575, Elizabeth I passed a law that removed benefit of clergy for all crimes. Only after conviction in a secular court could a person claim benefit of clergy to appeal for a more lenient punishment. This could still be granted to anyone who could recite the neck verse, clergyman or not.

> ### Revision Tip
> It is important that you keep track of both change and continuity across time periods.
>
> Create a table like the one below to map out change and continuity in law enforcement between the medieval and early modern periods.
>
> | | Continuity between the medieval and early modern periods | Change between the medieval and early modern periods |
> | --- | --- | --- |
> | Community law enforcement | | |
> | Authority law enforcement | | |

2.3 Punishment in early modern England

> **Research & Record**
>
> **To what extent did the nature of punishment change in the years c1500 to c1700?**
>
> Use pages 40 and 41 to complete a copy of this table. Record examples of change and continuity in punishment between the medieval and early modern periods.
>
> | Change | Continuity |
> |---|---|
> | | |

Continuity in punishment

During the period 1500–1700 the main aims of punishment continued to be retribution and deterrence. The methods used to punish those convicted of crime were mostly like those used in the medieval period too:

- Capital punishment was used for the most serious crimes. This was typically done by hanging – the punishment for people who were convicted of murder or witchcraft. Some heretics were burned at the stake. Being hanged, drawn and quartered was reserved for men found guilty of high treason.
- Executions were carried out in public as a deterrent to others.
- Corporal punishment such as mutilation, branding and whipping was used to punish less severe crimes such as vagabondage and drunkenness. This was also carried out in public and acted as a form of humiliation for the convicted criminal.
- Another form of public humiliation were the stocks and the pillory, which continued to be used in the early modern period.
- Fines continued to be the most common form of punishment and were used to punish minor offences such as failure to attend church, swearing or refusing to undertake the night watch.
- Prisoners awaiting trial were held in a secure room in an important building, such as a castle, rather than in purpose-built prisons.

Changes in punishment

During the early modern period, the authorities became increasingly worried about the crime rate, particularly for minor crimes. At the same time, the population continued to increase steadily. These two factors shaped new ideas, laws and punishments for crime.

Early prisons

While awaiting trial, prisoners were kept in poor and unsanitary conditions. Men, women and children were housed together and there was no separation of violent and petty criminals. Prisoners had to pay wardens for basic items such as food and bedding. However, by the mid-sixteenth century the authorities believed a new kind of prison might help cut crime rates.

In London, in 1556, the first house of correction was opened, called Bridewell Prison. It was used to punish poor people who had broken the law, such as vagabonds. It often housed the homeless and orphaned too. To pay for their keep, inmates were made to do hard labour. It was believed that this would **reform** their characters by encouraging the habit of work. Similar prisons were opened around the country during the seventeenth century.

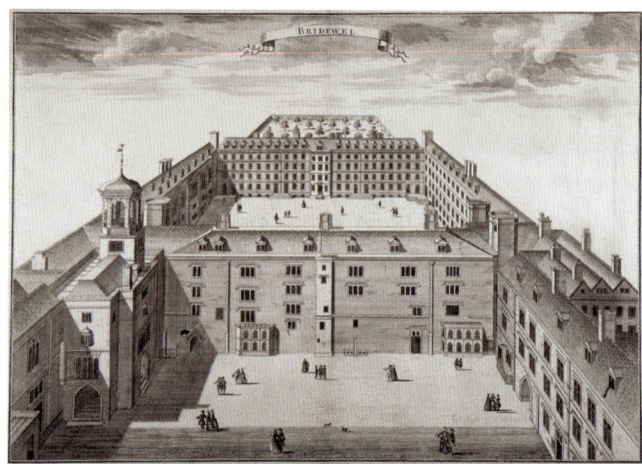

▲ An eighteenth-century engraving of Bridewell, a house of correction in London

Transportation

▲ A drawing of prisoners being taken to their ship for transportation to America in the 1700s

From the 1660s another new punishment was introduced, called **transportation**. Hangings peaked in around 1600, but the authorities were beginning to lose confidence in the deterrent effect of the death penalty and an increasing number of those sentenced to hang were pardoned. However, an alternative punishment was needed for those spared the noose, and transportation offered an alternative to hanging while ensuring the criminal no longer posed a threat to English society.

As England established more colonies in America, it began to transport some convicted criminals there. Once in America, convicted criminals were subject to unpaid labour, often in very harsh conditions. Some people believed that this would give criminals the chance to reflect on their crime and change their way of life. However, others were critical of transportation, believing that it was a soft option compared with the death penalty because the sentence was for a specific period of time, usually seven years.

The Bloody Code

The authorities also made changes to the law in response to concerns about the rising crime rate. Despite doubting its effectiveness as a deterrent, by 1688, the list of capital crimes (those that carried a death sentence) had increased to 50. Over the next 150 years, more crimes were added to the list until it reached its peak of 225 by 1815. Historians refer to this period as the '**Bloody Code**' because of the harsh attitude towards crime.

During the Bloody Code period, the death penalty was introduced for very specific offences, such as damaging Westminster Bridge. This made managing law enforcement and punishment difficult and executions were not always carried out. The significance of the Bloody Code lies with its symbolic value – it demonstrated the power of the authorities and their desire to get tough on crime.

2.4 Case study 1: The Gunpowder Plot

Research & Record

How far were responses to the Gunpowder Plot similar to responses to previous acts of treason?

In the exam, Question 3 tests your ability to compare two events or developments from different time periods. This activity will help you practise comparison.

1. How much can you remember about the crime of treason during the medieval period? Try to fill in the second column of a table like this from memory alone. Then, use your research notes and pages 40–41 to fill in any gaps.
2. Next, use pages 42–43 to fill in the third column.
3. Reflect on what you have found out:
   - Looking at the two time periods, what are the similarities in the nature of the crime of treason?
   - Are the responses from the authorities (punishment) similar?

	The medieval period c1000–c1500	The Gunpowder Plot
Factors that influenced the definition of treason		
Nature and purpose of punishment		

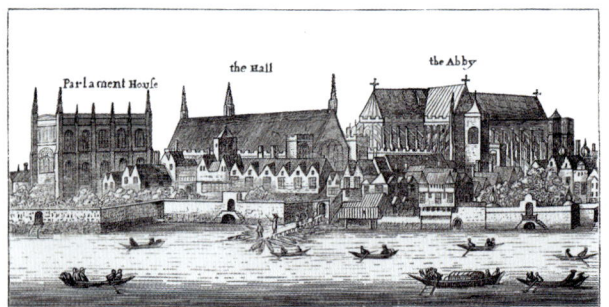

▲ The Houses of Parliament, 1605

The Houses of Parliament were considerably less grand in 1605 than they are today. However, their significance as a symbol of power and authority remained the same. When the Gunpowder Plotters developed a plan to blow up the Houses of Parliament, there was no mistaking that this was one of the biggest threats to power the monarchy had ever witnessed.

Why did the plotters want to blow up the Houses of Parliament?

By the 1600s England had experienced more than 60 years of religious turmoil as a result of Henry VIII's break from the Catholic Church in 1534. Life for English Catholics was particularly difficult under Elizabeth I.

After a 45-year reign, Elizabeth died in 1603 with no heirs of her own. English Catholics were hopeful that her Scottish cousin, King James VI of Scotland, would treat them with more tolerance when he came to the throne. James was a Protestant, but he was married to a Catholic and had a reputation for being a fair and wise ruler. However, he made it clear that nothing would change for Catholics in England under his rule and, in fact, laws preventing them from practising their faith were even more tightly enforced.

The plot

A man called Robert Catesby, who came from a family that had refused to accept the Protestant faith, gathered a small group of Catholic men, including Guy Fawkes (see page 30). On 20 May 1604, they met to discuss a plot to kill James I and the entire English political elite by blowing up the Houses of Parliament. They planned to replace him with a Catholic monarch or at least one who would be fairer to England's Catholics. The group rented a cellar directly beneath the House of Lords and Guy Fawkes was tasked with bringing in the gunpowder. The group planned to carry out their plot on 5 November 1605, when James I was due to give a speech for the ceremonial opening of parliament.

The failure of the plot

The plot had been badly organised and, on 20 October 1605, Lord Monteagle received a letter warning him not to attend parliament on 5 November. Fawkes was arrested on the night of 4 November. He was found guarding 36 barrels containing more than a ton of gunpowder below the Houses of Parliament.

Some historians believe that the authorities knew about the plot but allowed it to proceed so that the Catholic rebellion could be given publicity and their treatment of English Catholics could be justified.

▲ A drawing of some of the Gunpowder Plotters which was drawn soon after the plot was uncovered

Why were the Gunpowder Plotters punished so severely?

The remaining plotters were arrested in Staffordshire, having fled London when they heard the plot had been discovered. Robert Catesby was killed during the arrest, but the surviving plotters were found guilty of high treason and sentenced to be hanged, drawn and quartered.

The Gunpowder Plot was a serious threat to the authority of the king. Despite its failure, it was still high treason – the most serious of all crimes. James needed to ensure that his response to the plot deterred further attempts at rebellion. This is demonstrated through his decision to authorise the use of torture on Fawkes in order to reveal the names of the other plotters. Torture was rarely used in England and could only be authorised by the monarch or privy council (a group of advisors to the monarch who helped them govern).

Consequences of the plot

The plot had several consequences:

- The Thanksgiving Act ordered that 5 November become a day of commemoration each year.
- In 1606, Catholics were forced to take an oath of allegiance to the English Crown.
- Catholics were restricted from voting, becoming MPs or owning land in England. These laws were not repealed until 1829.

2.5 Case study 2: Matthew Hopkins

Research & Record

What factors enabled Matthew Hopkins to become the 'Witchfinder General'?

The table below shows a list of factors that allowed a surge in witch trials to take place in the seventeenth century. Use pages 44 and 45 to add information that explains the relevance of each factor. You may also find it useful to revisit your notes and pages 34–35 for additional information about the crime of witchcraft.

Factor	Explanation of relevance to Hopkins becoming 'Witchfinder General'
Individuals	
The Church	
The authorities	
Attitudes in society	
Scientific knowledge	

By the mid-1600s a series of unfortunate events led to further concern about witches. Crop failure because of the mini-ice age resulted in food shortages and inflation, a situation that was made worse by the outbreak of civil war. This created a climate in which accusations of witchcraft could flourish as people looked for **scapegoats** on whom to blame their misfortune.

The case of Elizabeth Clarke

In 1645, in Manningtree, Essex, a man named John Stearne was given a warrant by local magistrates to investigate claims of witchcraft committed by an elderly lady called Elizabeth Clarke. He invited 25-year-old Matthew Hopkins to be his assistant. According to Hopkins' book *The Discovery of Witches*, Hopkins had first become interested in witch-hunting after he overheard women discussing their meetings with the devil in 1644.

Witches were often assumed to be lone, elderly women on the fringes of society. Elizabeth Clarke was around 80 years old. She was a widow, had only one leg and was known in the local community to be bad tempered. She was accused of bewitching the wife of a local man when she suddenly became ill. Hopkins sent a group of women to Elizabeth Clarke's home, where she was stripped and searched. They were looking for the 'devil's mark', any scar, mole or birthmark

▲ A picture from Matthew Hopkins' book *The Discovery of Witches* that shows the case of Elizabeth Clarke

which was said to be proof of the witch's relationship with the devil. They found what they were looking for.

Clarke was then taken for interrogation as Hopkins wanted her confession. When Clarke would not confess, Hopkins used sleep deprivation to get it. Sleep deprivation was a legal method for collecting a confession because it was not classed as torture at the time. After three days and nights with no sleep, Clarke confessed to being a witch.

The Witchfinder General

Hopkins' success with Elizabeth Clarke encouraged him to hunt for more witches. He began operating in areas beyond the boundaries of his warrant and gave himself the title 'Witchfinder General'. As it turned out, Hopkins did not need to hunt very hard. He was invited into local communities that already had suspected witches and he was paid for each one found guilty. Between 1645 and 1647 approximately 300 cases of witchcraft were presented to the authorities in East Anglia and Essex, and at least 100 people were executed by hanging, most of them were women.

Hopkins continued to use sleep deprivation to get confessions and, on occasion, he was known to use the 'swim test', which involved the accused having their hands and feet bound, then being lowered into cold water by a rope around the waist. It was believed that the innocent would be accepted into the water and sink, whereas the guilty would be rejected and float.

The end of witch-hunting in England

Hopkins died of tuberculosis in 1647. His death reduced the number of witch accusations and trials in East Anglia and Essex. By 1650, economic hardship and crop failure were easing, and, in 1651, the civil war came to an end. Although some witch trials continued to take place, there were no more widespread panics over witches. Many of the factors that had created a climate for witch-hunting were no longer relevant and an increase in scientific thinking towards the end of the century helped people to understand the causes of misfortune rather than blaming witches. The last known execution for witchcraft was in 1714.

▲ Matthew Hopkins, the self-titled 'Witchfinder General'

2.6 Early modern period review

Review 1

Continuity and change

1. The period summary chart below summarises the early modern period. Study it carefully, then create a blank copy (with only the themes listed on the left-hand side) and try to reproduce all the information from memory alone. Use a whole page of A4 paper with three rows – one per theme. This is a challenge but worth the effort because it will reveal what you are able to remember easily and what you are finding harder to recall.
2. Once you have done the best you can, review your attempt against the period summary chart below. Fill in any gaps using a different coloured pen. This will remind you what you are struggling to remember.

Period summary c1500 to c1700		
Theme	**Evidence of continuity**	**Evidence of change**
Definitions of crime	• Crimes against the person were still considered serious crimes and were dealt with as they had been in the later medieval period. • There was no change in the way crimes against property were handled. • High treason was still considered to be the most serious of crimes against authority. • Poaching was still viewed by many as a social crime.	• The Reformation from 1534 changed attitudes towards crimes, including those against authority. • Heresy was a religious crime but became classed as a crime against authority because the monarch was head of the Church of England. • Religion was also a factor in the Gunpowder Plot and the rise of witchcraft as a significant crime. • There were new definitions of crime during this period with the introduction of laws against vagabondage, smuggling and witchcraft.
Enforcing the law	• The local community was still expected to join the hue and cry to chase down suspected criminals and bring them to justice. • Local men acting as parish constables were still expected to lead the hue and cry. • The role of justices of the peace continued.	• Watchmen were introduced in larger towns and cities. They kept watch for crime and arrested suspected criminals, including vagabonds. • Every male householder took a turn on the night watch. They patrolled at night with a lantern, bell and weapon to deter criminals. • There were changes in the use of benefit of clergy as monarchs continued to challenge the power and authority of church courts.
Punishment: deterrence, retribution and a move towards reform	• Punishment continued to be used for retribution and deterrence. • Capital punishment was used for the most serious crimes. Executions were carried out in public as a deterrent to others.	• Houses of correction and transportation were introduced as new forms of punishment. • Houses of correction were opened to deal with some crimes, such as vagabondage.

	• Corporal punishment such as whipping was used for less severe crimes. This was also carried out in public and acted as a form of humiliation for the convicted criminal. Mutilation and branding were also used as permanent public deterrents. • Another form of public humiliation were the stocks and pillory, which continued to be used in the early modern period. • Fines were the most common form of punishment. • Prisons were used to hold prisoners awaiting trial.	• Transportation was considered to be an alternative deterrent for serious crimes. It offered an alternative to the death penalty while removing criminals from English society. • Increased crime rates caused concern among the authorities and the number of crimes classed as capital crimes was increased. Historians refer to this legislation as the Bloody Code.

Review 2

What factors influenced crime and punishment in the years c1500 to c1700?

It is important to understand the factors that were influencing and driving change and continuity in each time period that you study. These factors are:

- attitudes in society
- the role of individuals
- the role of institutions, such as the Church and government
- science and technology.

The early modern period saw the emergence of some scientific thinking, which influenced the decline in witch trials by the end of the period. In addition, there is lots of evidence to support the roles played by society, individuals, government/authority and the Church during this period.

Using the information throughout this chapter, complete this table. Include specific names, dates or events to show what was influencing change and continuity across the early modern period.

Factor	How it influenced change	How it influenced continuity
Individuals		
Institutions: the Church		
Institutions: government/authority		
Attitudes in society		
Science and technology	More scientific thinking towards the end of the seventeenth century improved understanding of misfortune. This led to less scapegoating of witches and an end to mass witch hunts.	

Apply ▶ Exam Practice

Question 3 style

Explain **one** way in which punishment for the crime of treason in medieval England was different from punishment for the crime of treason in early modern England. (4 marks)

Look again at the advice on page 37 on answer question 3s. Remember to focus on difference.

2.7 Early modern period exam practice

> **Exam Tip**
>
> **Question 5/6: Judgement question**
>
> Questions 5 and 6 will ask you to make a judgement about how far you agree with a statement about causation, consequence, change, continuity or significance.
>
> Remember to use the **3Ds**:
>
> - **Decode** the question (work out the focus of the question).
> - **Decide** how to organise your answer into paragraphs.
> - **Develop** your answer by explaining and supporting the points you make.
>
> ---
>
> 'Religious change was the main reason that there were new definitions of crime in the period 1500–1700.'
> How far do you agree? Explain your answer. **(16 marks)**
>
> You may use the following in your answer:
> - heresy
> - vagabondage.
>
> You **must** also use information of your own.
>
> ---
>
> **What are the command words?**
> The question asks, 'How far do you agree?' You need to try to agree and disagree with the statement before reaching a judgement.
>
> **What is the conceptual focus?**
> The historical concept is significance. Describing religious change is not enough to get the higher-level marks. Focus on explaining why you agree and disagree that religious change influenced definitions of crime in the years c1500 to c1700 and then support with examples from your knowledge.
>
> **What is the content focus?**
> Focus on the role of religious change. Weigh this against other changes and developments during the early modern period, such as the role of individuals like James I. You need to include at least three aspects of knowledge throughout your answer.
>
> **How many marks are available?**
> '16 marks' indicates you should spend about 30 minutes on the question. You should try to write at least three paragraphs: at least one paragraph that agrees with the statement, at least one that disagrees and a conclusion.
>
> There are also 4 marks for SPaG, that means your spelling, punctuation and grammar. Check that you have spelled key terms, used capital letters, commas, full stops and paragraphs correctly.

> **Exam Tip**
>
> **Reaching a judgement**
>
> In the exam, you must reach a judgement about how far you agree with the statement. The easiest way to do this is to write a conclusion at the end of your answer. For example, when answering the question above:
>
> - Decide whether you agree or disagree that religious change was the most significant factor for new definitions of crime in the years c1500 to c1700 and begin your paragraph with *'In conclusion, religious change was / was not the main reason that there were new definitions in crime in the years c1500 to c1700 …'*.
> - Go on to explain why you have reached this judgement by weighing up how some definitions of crime, such as heresy, were influenced by religion, but other new crimes, such as vagabondage, were introduced by authorities responding to increased unemployment and homelessness.

Exam Tip

Use connectives and evidence for stronger arguments

When explaining why you agree and disagree with the statement, you have to prove your argument. For example:

> Religious change was the main reason for new definitions of crime in the period 1500–1700 because it created a period of religious upheaval and paranoia. For example, in 1534 Henry VIII broke from the Catholic Church and established the Church of England. This meant that people had to swear the Oath of Supremacy, accepting Henry as head of the Church. This led to some people breaking the law because of their religious beliefs. Heresy was the crime of holding religious beliefs that had been banned. Religious change also had an impact on treason during the early modern period. High treason was already a very serious crime against authority, but after the Reformation there was an increase in rebellion and this led to the Gunpowder Plot in 1605. The plotters wanted to remove James I from the throne and replace him with a Catholic monarch. This demonstrates the impact of religious change in the years c1500 to c1700.

Use connectives to tie what you know to the statement

Phrases like 'this meant that', 'this led to' and 'this resulted in' are called connectives because they tie what you know to the statement and so help you prove your argument.

Add specific knowledge

Provide evidence to substantiate (support) your argument. Use phrases such as 'for example', 'such as' and 'this demonstrates' to introduce or flag your supporting evidence.

Apply ▶ Exam Practice

Question 5/6 style

'There was little change in the nature of punishment in the years c1000 to c1700.'

How far do you agree? Explain your answer. (16 marks)

You may use the following in your answer:
- deterrence
- transportation.

You **must** also use information of your own.

Use the Exam Tips on page 48 and above to help you with tackling this question.

Exam Tip

Check the dates

Check the dates in the question carefully to make sure that you are writing about the correct chronological period in the history of crime and punishment in Britain. This question refers to c1000 to c1700, so you need to use your knowledge of punishment in both the medieval and early modern periods.

Part 3 c1700–c1900: Crime and punishment in eighteenth- and nineteenth-century Britain

Connect and Engage – Michael Barrett

Who was Michael Barrett?

Michael Barrett was born in Ireland in 1841. He was an Irish activist and belonged to a group called the Irish Republican Brotherhood, also known as the Fenians, who campaigned for Ireland's independence from the United Kingdom.

An explosion

On 13 December 1867 members of the Irish Republican Brotherhood set off an explosion at Clerkenwell Prison in London. They were attempting to free a senior Fenian imprisoned there, called Ricard O'Sullivan Burke. The explosion destroyed a large section of the prison wall and badly damaged several houses opposite the prison. It killed 12 people and wounded approximately 120 more. Burke did not escape. The Clerkenwell bombing was the largest act of violence carried out by the Irish Republican Brotherhood in mainland Britain.

▲ Michael Barrett on the scaffold. This was the last execution at Newgate prison, in 1868.

Why is Michael Barrett significant?

Michael Barrett was arrested and put on trial for the bombing. Witnesses for Barrett testified that he had been in Scotland on the date of the explosion. However, other witnesses claimed that Barrett had told them that he had participated in the plan. The jury found him guilty. He was hanged outside Newgate Prison on 26 May 1868 in front of a hostile crowd of up to 2000 people, who booed and sang 'Rule Britannia' during his execution.

We can learn a lot from Michael Barrett's story about the nature of punishment and attitudes of society during this period. Barrett's execution was the last public hanging to take place in England. After 1868 hangings were to be carried out behind prison walls. For centuries public executions had been a key feature of deterrence punishment, but as Barrett's case shows, crowds were becoming larger and more problematic to control.

The reaction of the crowd at Barrett's execution also helps us understand how immigration was causing tension during this period. Whitechapel, which was in the East End of London (see Key Topic 5), was experiencing high numbers of Irish and Jewish immigrants during the nineteenth century. This contributed to the existing social problems, including increasing competition for jobs, overcrowding and suspicion within communities. Racism, in particular anti-Irish prejudice, and both anti-Catholic and antisemitic religious bigotry led people to blame immigrants for problems that had much wider causes.

Connect & Engage

What can the story of Michael Barrett tell us about changing attitudes to crime and punishment in the eighteenth and nineteenth centuries?

1. Give one reason why public executions were stopped from 1868.
2. Explain how immigration increased tension within some communities during the period.
3. What impact might this have had on attitudes towards criminals and crime?

3.1 Understanding the eighteenth and nineteenth centuries

A changing society

During this period, Britain experienced high population growth. The population of England and Wales in 1750 was 9.5 million, but this had increased to 41.5 million by 1900. Urbanisation meant that most people now lived in towns and cities rather than in the countryside.

There were also political changes which enabled most men to vote, rather than just the wealthy. As a result, the government started to intervene on issues such as preventing crime and catching criminals to try to secure the votes of ordinary people. By the end of the nineteenth century, most people accepted that the government should have some control over local affairs and address social problems and domestic issues.

An industrial revolution

From around 1750 Britain became the first country in the world to industrialise. New factories and methods for producing materials such as iron and steel were changing the way that people worked and the speed at which goods could be produced. Towns and cities grew around these new industries and people flocked into them. Cheap housing, often constructed quickly and poorly, was built to accommodate the rising and Britain's industrial towns soon developed a reputation for being gloomy, overcrowded, unhealthy and stricken with poverty.

The impact on crime, punishment and law enforcement

The period 1700–1900 saw some massive changes to crime and punishment. Society was changing rapidly and as society changed, so did people's attitudes towards crime and punishment. Poverty led to an increase in crime against property, but violent crime, particularly murder decreased. This was because changing societal attitudes created an intolerance for violence. It was this attitude shift that challenged centuries-old ideas about using harsh corporal and capital punishments as deterrents and a discussion began about the best way to deal with criminals. Also, for the first time in history, a full-time and professional police force was established.

▲ Smoking chimneys dominate the Manchester skyline in 1870

> **Revision Tip**
>
> Understanding the changes to a society is an important part of knowing how attitudes within that society were shaped. Using the information on this page, create a flow diagram which demonstrates how the Industrial Revolution and the wider changes in British society at the time, such as population increase, affected attitudes to crime and punishment during the eighteenth and nineteenth centuries.

3.2 Changing definitions of criminal activity c1700–c1900

Research & Record

To what extent did definitions of crime change during the period 1700–1900?

Use pages 52–55 to complete a copy of this table. Write a description of each crime and identify whether this demonstrates continuity or change from the early modern period. Use the 'Explain' column to provide evidence in support of your choice.

Criminal activity	Description	Continuity	Change	Explain
Witchcraft	People were believed to be working with the devil to cause harm or misfortune to others.		✓	Religious turmoil was no longer a concern and, in 1736, a change to the law meant witchcraft was no longer a crime.
Heresy				
Vagabondage				
Theft				
Highway robbery				
Poaching				
Smuggling				

Change and continuity in definitions of crime 1700–1900

Heresy and witchcraft

During the early modern period (c1500–c1700), fears over the crimes of heresy and witchcraft had been fuelled by significant religious change as a result of the Reformation and this period of religious instability had increased tension within communities. However, by the eighteenth century these fears had passed. The last execution for heresy took place in 1612 and, although the final execution for witchcraft didn't happen until just over 100 years later, in 1714, a change to the law in 1736 meant that witchcraft was no longer considered a crime by the mid-eighteenth century. This law change was helped greatly by the establishment of the Royal Society, which was approved by Charles II in 1660. The Society aimed to improve understanding of the natural world through new scientific thinking. As a result, misfortunes that previously had been blamed on witches, such as failed crops, were explained in other ways. This increased scientific knowledge was supported by greater religious stability and a general decline in the belief that the supernatural could influence day-to-day life.

Vagabondage

However, concern over vagrancy continued during the eighteenth and nineteenth centuries. While the Industrial Revolution led to Britain becoming wealthier, it also meant it was far more common for people to move around the country to find work in new industries and factories. Employment levels fluctuated and some people found themselves unemployed because new machinery had taken their place. So, there were high levels of economic insecurity among the working classes and many people living in towns and cities lived in poverty. New vagrancy laws were passed in both the eighteenth and nineteenth centuries, which were used to tackle the resulting begging and disorderly behaviour.

While some fears over religion and witchcraft declined, the authorities found new reasons for concern that impacted the definition of crime in the period 1700–1900. They were concerned about activity that disrupted trade, or threatened the interests of landowners and factory owners, because these things threatened the prosperity of Britain's new thriving industries.

Theft

Theft continued to be common. However, different types of goods were stolen and the methods used for theft began to change. Theft from the workplace, particularly the docks, was becoming a concern.

Petty theft, particularly pickpocketing, thrived in towns and cities where large populations meant it was easier to commit this crime and evade capture.

There was also an increase in the theft of more valuable goods, such as clothing, pottery and cutlery. Thieves targeted canal boats, which were a popular form of transport at the start of the Industrial Revolution, and coaches and wagons on the roads which were used for moving people and goods from town to town. This type of theft was known as **highway robbery**.

Highway robbery

Highway robbery was not a new crime; it had been a problem as far back as the Middle Ages but, by the early 1700s, it was becoming a bigger problem for several reasons.

- Travel between towns and cities increased because of greater trade and new, better-quality roads. This increase in travellers provided more opportunity for highwaymen to strike, and quieter, isolated country roads between towns and cities were ideal for robberies to take place.
- It was usual for people to carry their money and valuables with them as banks were not commonly used at this time.
- Increased trade and the Industrial Revolution led to an increase in the movement of valuable goods around the country.

Highway robbers were usually armed and on horseback. They targeted carriages carrying wealthy travellers and forced them to hand over their valuables. Highway robbery was greatly feared and the authorities were concerned about the disruption it caused to trade. Highway robbery had been a capital offence (punished by the death penalty) for a long time but, in 1772, it became a capital offence to be armed and in disguise on the road.

Some highwaymen became well known and popularised through the media at the time. One of them, James MacLaine, had a reputation for being a gentleman. But highway robbery was, in some cases, a brutal and violent crime.

However, by the 1830s the crime of highway robbery was in decline. The growth of the banking system meant that there was less need for people to carry large sums of cash, and the introduction of mounted patrols to protect the highways and travellers is believed to have deterred some highwaymen.

▲ A contemporary image of the eighteenth-century highwayman James MacLaine robbing Lord Elgington on Hounslow Heath, west of London

Smuggling

As we have seen, smuggling started to become an issue during the early modern period. But by the eighteenth century it had developed into a massive problem in coastal areas. It was fast becoming an organised crime, with large gangs of smugglers such as the Hawkhurst Gang bringing in items such as tea, cloth and alcohol without paying import duties. In the days before income tax, the government relied heavily upon these taxes as a main source of income and therefore it took this crime very seriously. Smuggling was one of the crimes listed under the Bloody Code, which meant that those caught faced the death penalty.

However, it remained difficult to catch smugglers despite improved efforts to do so. The government introduced a coastline patrol, but smugglers found it relatively easy to give the patrols the slip because they usually worked at night under cover of darkness, there were not enough patrols and they had to cover large areas. In addition, smuggling was generally still considered to be a social crime. Smugglers were protected by the communities in which they lived, and people didn't report cases of smuggling because they benefited from lower-priced goods. In fact, many smugglers relied upon a network of ordinary people to carry out their work, as they assisted in hiding, moving and selling the smuggled goods.

By the 1840s smuggling was in decline because the government reduced taxes on many of the goods that smugglers brought into the country illegally and therefore smuggling was no longer as profitable.

▲ The Hawkhurst Gang raid the King's Custom House in Poole to retrieve their confiscated smuggled goods in 1747

Poaching

In both the medieval and early modern periods, the public viewed poaching as a social crime that did no one any harm. The authorities, meanwhile, classed poaching as a very serious crime. In the medieval period the Forest Laws made poaching a crime against authority, and similarly the Game Act of 1671 was introduced to protect the land of the wealthy during the early modern period.

During the eighteenth and nineteenth centuries attitudes towards poaching remained largely the same, although the government stepped up efforts to catch and bring poachers to justice. In 1773, the Waltham Black Act was introduced. It aimed to deal with an increase in poaching, particularly the rise of large-scale poaching gangs. The law made it a criminal offence for a person to carry weapons in hunting areas and to disguise their face – it was common for poachers to dirty their faces to become less noticeable and unrecognisable. Armed gamekeepers were introduced to protect the land and to catch poachers, who faced the death sentence under the new law.

However, public sympathy for poachers remained the same as it had been previously. Most poachers were still poor people hunting for food to feed their families and people felt the new law was unfair and too harsh in its use of the death penalty. Villagers often lied in court to protect poachers from conviction.

Revision Tip

In this section, you will have noticed that some crimes are very similar to crimes you have learned about in the previous sections of this book, whereas others are new.

As you learn about and reflect on changing definitions of crime in Britain from c1000 to the present day, look for change and continuity. You can organise your notes in a table similar to the one here.

Changing definitions of crime in Britain, c1000–present	
Examples of change	Examples of continuity

Think about why attitudes to punishment changed using the following factors:
- individuals
- the role of the Church
- the role of government/authorities
- science and technology
- attitudes in society.

New definitions of crime c1700–c1900

The Tolpuddle Martyrs

In 1789, the French people rebelled and overthrew their monarchy in an event which came to be known as the French Revolution. The revolution was a demonstration of the power of the masses and the British government of the time was concerned that a similar revolution could occur in Britain. This fear influenced some of its decisions about law and order.

The government was particularly concerned about protests and for this reason it kept a close eye on trade unions. Trade unions are groups of people who work within a particular industry and aim to protect the rights of workers by campaigning for better working conditions and fair pay. Trade unions themselves and belonging to a trade union was not illegal, but some employers became concerned that having a union could cause disruption or be a threat to their business.

In 1833, a group of six farm labourers from the village of Tolpuddle in Dorset asked their employers for a pay increase. They believed this was a fair request because they had been given several pay cuts. The farm owners rejected the request and, in response, the six men decided to form a trade union to help them campaign more effectively. Other farm workers heard about the union and wanted to join. They wanted a guarantee that there would be no further pay cuts. Union members were asked to pay a joining fee and to swear an oath of loyalty.

The government was concerned by the increasing popularity of trade unions, and wanted to deter others from joining. So, they turned to an old navy law which made it illegal to swear a secret oath. This is an example of how the government was able to change the definition of crime for its own purposes. Swearing an oath to join a trade union was therefore a crime.

In 1834, the leaders of the Tolpuddle union were charged with swearing a secret oath because they had asked members to swear an oath of loyalty. They were found guilty at trial and sentenced to seven years of transportation to a penal colony in Australia, the maximum sentence possible for their crime. The severity of the punishment shows the extent to which the authorities wanted to deter others from forming trade unions.

The men became known as the **Tolpuddle Martyrs** for standing up for union rights. Some unions did disband for fear of receiving the same treatment, so it could be argued that the government was successful in achieving its aim of reducing union activity. But many more were outraged by the way the Tolpuddle Martyrs had been treated and a petition demanding the release of the men was signed by 250,000 people. There were also several protests about their treatment which attracted large crowds, and this concerned the government more. In 1836, the Tolpuddle Martyrs were granted a pardon and allowed to return home after serving two years of their sentence.

▲ A contemporary drawing of four of the six agricultural labourers who became known as the Tolpuddle Martyrs

Connect & Engage

What can we learn about attitudes to crime and punishment c1700–c1900 from the treatment of the Tolpuddle Martyrs?

What was the Todpuddle Martyrs' crime? How were they punished? Do you think the punishment was proportional to the crime committed?

Add a row to the Research & Record table you started on page 52 for 'Trade union activity'.

Revision Tip

It is important that you know the nature (the type) of crime committed and can make judgements about why these definitions might or might not change during each of the time periods you study. This is also important in understanding the bigger picture and identifying change and continuity between one time period and another.

Consider how definitions for different types of crime have changed so far. Create a table to map out change and continuity in definitions of crime from the medieval period to 1900. Provide an example of each crime alongside their definitions.

	Definition in medieval period c1000–c1500 and example	Definition in early modern period c1500–c1700 and example	Definition in eighteenth and nineteenth centuries c1700–c1900 and example
Crimes against authority			
Crimes against the person			
Crimes against property			

3.3 The nature of law enforcement c1700–c1900

Research & Record

Why were there changes in law enforcement during the eighteenth century?

Complete the table below using the information on this page and on page 59.

Think carefully about the language you use to state how important each reason was. In column 2, choose a word or phrase from the scale on the right to show the level of importance. Do not fill in column 3 if you think a reason had no or only minimal impact.

Essential	No change could have happened without it
Important	Without it change might have been less widespread or significant
Minimal	Had only a little impact
No importance	No influence at all

Reason	Importance	Explanation
The growth of towns and cities		
New opportunities for crime		
The Bow Street Runners		

Increasing crime rates

The period c1700–c1900 saw huge developments in methods of policing and law enforcement from the eighteenth century because the government needed to get on top of increasing crime rates. The increasing amount of crime was due to many people moving to live in towns and cities, which increased the opportunities for crime and made old enforcement methods ineffective and also caused increased poverty.

Towns
The populations of towns grew with industrialisation, so communities were less tight-knit and people no longer knew each other in the same way.

Opportunity
More people meant greater opportunity for crime. The old law enforcement methods, such as parish constables, town watchmen and the hue and cry, became less effective and communities were not able to police themselves as they had before.

Poverty
More people also led to more poverty. With no work security and harsh living conditions, many people had to resort to crime in order to survive.

Summarise

Remember the causes of increasing crime rates that resulted in changes to law enforcement during the eighteenth century using the acronym **TOP**, because the government needed to get on TOP of increasing crime rates.

Towns
Opportunity
Poverty

The Bow Street Runners

In 1749, the Bow Street Runners were founded by Henry Fielding, who was Chief Magistrate at Bow Street Magistrates Court in London. He wanted more men on the streets to reduce crime. Initially, he recruited six men to act as detectives and to apprehend criminals in the Bow Street area, but this number soon expanded to include a larger area with more men and a horse patrol to tackle highway robbery. In 1754, Henry died and his brother John Fielding, also a magistrate, took over the Bow Street Runners.

The Bow Street Runners were thief-takers, which meant that they earned money from rewards paid by the state (and sometimes the victim) for convicting criminals. Individual thief-takers were becoming more popular around the country, but were often corrupt, initiating false prosecutions to earn the rewards. Henry Fielding was the first person to tackle this corruption by organising them into a paid, unified force. Initially their impact was limited as they operated only in a small area of London, but by the 1770s their activities covered most of London, and from 1785 the government took over payment of their wage, making them the first modern police force.

The Bow Street Runners were a significant turning point in law enforcement. The Fielding brothers recognised the importance of collecting and sharing information with other law enforcement teams. They also published a magazine called 'The Hue and Cry', which contained information about criminals, crimes and stolen goods, and their office on Bow Street became a hub for crime intelligence.

Thanks to the Fielding brothers, a more organised system of preventing crime had developed in London by 1800, but there was still no overall co-ordination of constables, watchmen and runners. Many feared the cost of a police force and worried the government might use it to limit people's freedoms.

Perhaps most importantly, the Bow Street Runners proved that an organised and government-supported police force could increase criminal prosecution rates, paving the way for the first professional police force in 1829.

▲ Bow Street Runners in action, capturing two muggers, 1806. (The Bow Street Runners are wearing blue and green tailcoats.)

The development of a professional police force

Research & Record

Why was there a need for a professional police force by 1829?

Read pages 60 and 61 to gather evidence to support the arguments in the table. You will be able to use these notes to answer an exam question later in this section.

Argument	Support
Crime rates were increasing	This happened because …
Old systems of law enforcement were ineffective	Parish constables and town watchmen were no longer effective because …
There was increased government concern about civilian unrest/revolution	An example of this took place at …
The Bow Street Runners had proved that a more organised system of law enforcement could be effective	The Bow Street Runners were successful at …
A new police force would be more effective than the army or the Bow Street Runners	Their duties and appearance were distinctively different because …

Reasons for the introduction of a police force

By the nineteenth century, there was significant growing concern about crime rates, which had increased for several reasons:

- In 1815 new taxes known as the 'Corn Laws' were introduced for the import of grain. This led to higher food prices.
- Poverty rates had increased.
- Unemployment was rising.
- As a result, there were large-scale protests, which increased government concern about a revolution.

It was clear that a system of parish constables and town watchmen was no longer adequate and from the mid-eighteenth century the work of the Fielding brothers had demonstrated that an organised force of men could be effective in tackling crime. In extreme cases the army was used to deal with protest, but an event in 1819 had shown the army were not appropriately trained to police public protest.

The Peterloo Massacre

In 1819, around 60,000 working-class people gathered at St Peter's Field in Manchester to campaign to make voting fairer and more equal. The relatively peaceful protest became a disaster after the local magistrate instructed the Yeomanry (a volunteer cavalry unit who were part of the army reserve) to break up the meeting. Around 18 people were killed and hundreds injured when the cavalrymen charged into the crowd on horseback.

People were angry that a military force had been used on peaceful protesters and the event became known as the Peterloo Massacre. Although it was common at the time to call on these part-time soldiers to deal with protests and riots, it demonstrated the need for a more effective force to deal with such matters.

▲ The Yeomanry, wearing a distinctively military-style uniform, enter St Peter's Field, Manchester, to deal with protesters in 1819

A turning point: the first professional police force

◀ Some of Robert Peel's new police force, known as Peelers, c1870

In 1829, Sir Robert Peel gained government backing for the Metropolitan Police Act, which introduced an official, government-backed police force in London.

Peel wanted his new police force to be distinctively different from the army. He knew that there was public concern after the Peterloo Massacre and that a great number of people were resistant to the idea of a government-backed police force. To try to gain public confidence in his new police force, Peel introduced:

- a uniform of blue overcoats and top hats that looked more like civilian than military clothing
- 'beats' which became official walking routes that officers followed each day to deter criminals, similar to what watchmen had done.

However, for many people the idea of greater government control and involvement in their daily lives was still unwelcome as they feared that it would affect their freedoms, such as their right to protest. There was concern that the police would be an oppressive, military-style force on the streets and, as a result, Peel's new police force faced criticism and hostility from the public and the press.

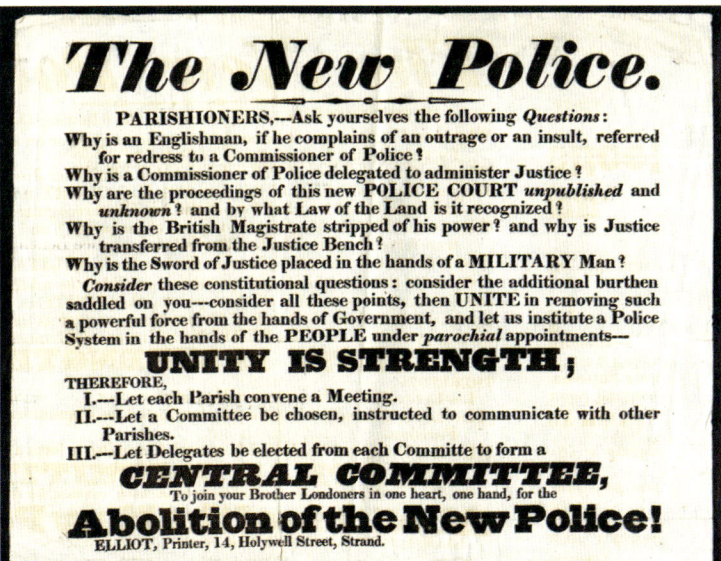

▲ A poster from 1830 calls for the 'Abolition of the New Police'

Connect & Engage

Where can you see evidence of the public opposition to the introduction of the Metropolitan Police Force in this poster?

Developments in policing after 1829

Research & Record

What contribution did the new police force make to law enforcement during the nineteenth century?

The table below shows the approaches to law enforcement before the introduction of the Metropolitan Police Force in 1829. Copy the table and complete the right-hand column with details of changes to law enforcement after the introduction of the new police force as you read pages 62–63.

Law enforcement before the introduction of the Metropolitan Police Force	Changes after the introduction of the Metropolitan Police Force and their significance
A local rather than a national concern	
No communication between different regions, which made it harder to catch criminals on the move	
Parish constables and town watchmen were untrained and had no uniform	
The standard of law enforcement varied from region to region	
Relied heavily on deterrence	

The creation of the Metropolitan Police Force was a significant turning point in the policing of London. But outside the capital city many of the same problems existed and there were huge differences in policing from region to region. Some regions embraced the idea of a new police force. In the North of England, the city of Carlisle was one of many towns and cities to have a fully regulated police force and, in 1837, the city employed Britain's first black police officer, John Kent. However, some others relied upon the old system of parish constables or town watchmen.

Change was slow for several reasons:

- Until 1856 new laws regarding police forces were optional rather compulsory, so regions outside of London were not obliged to introduce their own police forces.
- Many places still saw policing as a local rather than a national concern.
- Fears over the cost and resistance to the intrusion of a police force continued.

Developments after 1856

The 1856 Police Act made it compulsory for all towns and counties to set up professional police forces that would be locally controlled but supervised by the government. To reduce fears over the costs to local people, the new forces would receive government financial grants, but to do so they had to prove they were delivering police services efficiently and checks were carried out by government officials.

The Act was a significant move aimed at deterring criminals on a nationwide scale. It was thought that uniformed police officers walking the beat would deter would-be criminals by being visible, a method known as crime **prevention**.

In 1869, the first National Crime Records were established, which greatly improved communication between regions. This enabled different forces to effectively share details about crime and suspects.

The CID – from deterrence to detection

Most of the law enforcement methods used in the medieval period, the early modern period and at the beginning of the eighteenth century had relied on the concept of deterrence and prevention (for example watchmen). Deterrence had been reinforced by harsh punishments.

Crime detection (the finding of a criminal and presenting of evidence) had always existed, but until the Bow Street Runners, the first detectives to place crime detection at the centre of their role, the emphasis had often been on the victim or the local community to find the criminal and present evidence for the court.

In 1842, a detective branch was established at Scotland Yard. It had 16 officers and they investigated crimes and patrolled the streets in plain clothes rather than in uniform. In 1878, the **Criminal Investigation Department (CID)** was set up. It was established for investigative police work which, before forensic science, meant gathering evidence, taking photographs and interviewing witnesses.

The CID played a role in trying to identify Jack the Ripper during 1888, and in 1902 they secured the first fingerprint conviction, of a man called Harry Jackson whose fingerprints were used to convict him for burglary.

> ### Revision Tip
>
> **Metropolitan Police mnemonic**
>
> A good memory aid summarises the key points in as few words as possible and has a mnemonic or a drawing to help trigger memory.
>
> **A = Army** Peel wanted a uniform that was civilian rather than resembling that of the army
>
> **B = Beats** The set routes walked by police officers to deter criminals
>
> **C = Crime prevention** A visible uniformed police force supported crime prevention
>
> **D = Detection** The establishment of the CID allowed police to work in crime detection
>
> **E = Expansion** The success of the Metropolitan Police Force led to compulsory expansion of uniformed policing around the country from 1856

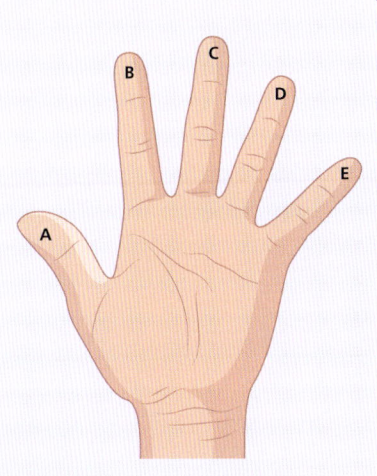

▲ The ABCDE of the Metropolitan Police

3.4 Changing views on the purpose of punishment c1700–c1900

Research & Record

Why did attitudes to punishment change during the period 1700–1900?

Use pages 64–65 to complete a copy of this table. Write a description for each punishment and identify how changing attitudes at the time led to the change in the use of the punishment.

Punishment	Description	Evidence of changing attitudes
Transportation		
Public execution		
The Bloody Code		

The end of transportation, public execution and the Bloody Code

Transportation

After the outbreak of the American War of Independence in 1776, Britain was unable to continue transporting convicts to America. Australia became the new destination as Britian began its colonisation of the continent from 1788. It was hoped that this would help secure Australia for Britain and that the hard work undertaken by criminals once there would reform their characters. It also fulfilled the need for a substantial alternative to the death penalty, which the authorities were losing confidence in as an effective deterrent.

In the penal colony, convicts had to perform hard labour in return for food, clothes and shelter. If they refused they were given the death penalty. At the end of their sentence many convicts could not afford the passage back to Britain so stayed in Australia.

Transportation was used for crimes such as theft or political protest. A large number of people transported had originally been sentenced to death but were given pardons on condition of transportation.

However, by the mid-nineteenth century the use of transportation was becoming problematic and it was discontinued as a punishment in 1868. This happened for several reasons:

- Gold had been discovered in Australia, making it an attractive destination for non-criminals who emigrated with hopes of finding their fortunes. Therefore, this weakened the deterrent effect of transportation.

- Colonists began to protest about criminals being sent to their country and Britain needed to keep them happy in order to maintain control of Australia.

- Prisons were being used more widely, meaning criminals could now be sentenced to time behind bars instead of transportation. This was cheaper than the cost of transporting them.
- There was still debate about the effectiveness of transportation. Some felt it wasn't a good enough deterrent, whereas others believed it was too harsh.

Public execution

For centuries, **public execution** had been a key feature of deterrence. However, throughout the nineteenth century the government became concerned about the behaviour of the large crowds that public hangings attracted. These concerns arose from a number of factors:

- There was a risk of protest and rioting.
- At a time of industrial growth and prosperity, some employers were annoyed that their factories had to close on execution day.
- Rather than being a deterrent, public hangings encouraged further crime. Pickpockets were attracted to the large crowds and outbreaks of fighting and violence were not uncommon.
- Attitudes to the death penalty were beginning to change. Some people felt it was too harsh a punishment. They wanted punishments that fitted the crime.

The last public execution took place on 26 May 1868 (see page 50). The use of hanging continued well into the twentieth century, with executions taking place in private, typically inside prisons.

The Bloody Code

By 1815, 225 crimes had been named as capital crimes. A conviction for one of these crimes carried the death sentence, which has led to historians referring to the laws that mandated death as the 'Bloody Code'.

The print entitled 'Merry England' (right) was produced by William Heath in 1831. It uses satire to show the impact of the use of harsh punishments during the Swing Riots of 1830, during which agricultural labourers were harshly punished for their protests over their poor wages and living standards and the introduction of new farm machinery which led to increased unemployment. 'Merry England' was a popular sentimental term at the time that referred to a prosperous and powerful England during the nineteenth century, yet the image demonstrates how, throughout the period that historians refer to as the Bloody Code, the authorities consistently used harsh punishment as a method of maintaining control over the population.

Despite this there had been no decrease in the crime rate and juries were reluctant to find criminals guilty of minor crimes knowing that they would be sentenced to death. This resulted in some petty crimes going unpunished. The Bloody Code was not acting as the successful deterrent the authorities had hoped it would.

Throughout the 1820s, Sir Robert Peel convinced parliament to make several changes to law, which included a significant reduction in the number of crimes punishable by death. This effectively ended the Bloody Code, though the most serious offences, such as murder and treason, were still punishable by death.

▲ 'Merry England' by William Heath (1831). The image uses satire to show the impact of the Bloody Code

Prison reform

Research & Record

How did campaigners for prison reform influence the 1823 Gaols Act?

Use pages 66–67 to complete your own copy of this table. Identify the problems that were found within prisons and how the ideas and work of John Howard and Elizabeth Fry influenced changes.

Problem	How the ideas of Howard and Fry influenced change
Children not separated from adult criminals	Elizabeth Fry introduced basic schooling in prisons for children to help reform them

For centuries cells or 'gaols' (pronounced 'jail') had been used to detain criminals awaiting trial. But using detention as a method of punishment and reform was not considered until the introduction of houses of correction in the early modern period.

However, changing attitudes towards punishment meant that, by the late nineteenth century, prison had become the most common form of punishment.

Early prisons

Early prisons looked and felt different from the kind of prison system we are familiar with today. In typical prisons there were various issues:

- Cells often housed multiple people at any one time.
- There was very limited separation of offenders, meaning that often those who had committed serious crimes were kept alongside first-time offenders or those who had committed minor offences.
- Men and women were not separated during the day, though often were at night.
- Children were not separated from adults. This earned prisons a reputation as 'schools for crime' as the young or inexperienced criminals often learned from older, more experienced criminals.
- Prison wardens were not paid, which meant they were open to bribery. Prisoners with money could purchase themselves a considerably better experience inside than those prisoners who were poor.
- The diet was poor (unless you were rich) and the accommodation was dirty, damp and poorly ventilated. This made disease and illness a huge problem. Common illnesses were typhus and dysentery, which were caused by drinking dirty water.

It took years of campaigning and reform to create modern prisons and tackle the issues that early prisons presented.

Prison reform

During the 1820s, Sir Robert Peel began a process of **penal reform** – changes to the way that punishment operated in society. He advocated for a system that reformed criminals and prevented crime, rather than one of pure deterrence. As a result, the 1823 Gaols Act was introduced, which improved conditions in prisons for prisoners.

The Act was heavily influenced by individuals who campaigned for change, such as Elizabeth Fry and John Howard.

The work of John Howard

As the sheriff of Bedfordshire John Howard inspected local prisons. He was outraged by the unclean conditions at Bedfordshire County Gaol. Howard visited other prisons looking for a good example on which to remodel the gaol in Bedfordshire. He was not able to find one. In fact, conditions were so bad that, in 1777, he published his findings in a document titled 'The state of prisons in England and Wales'.

Howard argued that prisoners could only change their ways if prison conditions were healthier, including clean cells and a better diet. He firmly believed that prisons should offer useful work, Christian teachings and places for reflection. Additionally, he campaigned for prison wardens to be paid to put an end to bribery.

Howard was criticised at the time for being too lenient on criminals. But there were other campaigners who supported his ideas.

The work of Elizabeth Fry

Elizabeth Fry was a Quaker and had been involved in charity work since the age of 18. Her work took her to Newgate Prison in London. She discovered prisoners who had been detained without trial and in filthy, overcrowded living conditions. In particular, she was horrified to see women and children living alongside dangerous male criminals.

She campaigned for improved living conditions for all prisoners, but she particularly advocated for better treatment of women and their children. Concerned at the way male wardens treated female prisoners, she helped ensure that female wardens were employed. Similarly, she also advocated for the separation of male and female prisoners for their safety. She also established basic schooling for children and bible classes to encourage rehabilitation of prisoners through religious teaching, as well as education and employment opportunities for female prisoners.

Like Howard, she was criticised for her lenient attitude towards punishment. However, she continued to press for prison reform by writing campaign letters to the government. Her work influenced the 1823 Gaols Act.

Summarise ✓

Aids to remembering key information

Use this mnemonic (or one of your own) to help you remember changes to punishments throughout the nineteenth century.

By the end of the nineteenth century the government had overcome **HEAPS** of problems with punishment:

H = **Howard** published his findings on prisons in England and Wales, highlighting major concerns

E = **Elizabeth Fry** campaigned for prison reform and influenced the 1823 Gaols Act

A = **Australia** was no longer used for transportation after the punishment ended in 1868

P = **Prisons** became the most common form of punishment and conditions began to improve

S = **Sentences** for death were carried out privately after the practice of public execution ended in 1868

▲ An engraving of Elizabeth Fry reading to the women prisoners of Newgate Prison in 1816

3.5 Case study 1: Pentonville Prison

Research & Record

What can we learn from the building of Pentonville Prison about changing attitudes towards punishment in Britain c1700–c1900?

1 Copy and complete this table using pages 68–70. Provide examples and descriptions of conditions in Pentonville in column 2 and explain how each of these reflected changing attitudes to punishment in Britain.

	Example/Description	How this reflected changing attitudes
The separate system		
Work		
Facilities		
Living conditions		

2 Why were there criticisms of Pentonville Prison from people such as Elizabeth Fry?

A new type of prison

Through the work of individual campaigners and government reform, the prison system was slowly starting to develop into one that was tough but did not risk the health of its prisoners.

Between 1842 and 1877, the government built 90 new prisons. Pentonville was the first, designed and built as a prototype where a new type of imprisonment called the **separate system** could be tested. It was designed to deter criminals, but also to reform them.

Pentonville had five wings which were made up of individual cells and could house 520 prisoners in total. Cells were small, with a singular high window to allow for some daylight. The prison featured some of the most up-to-date technology, including clean, piped water to each cell which supplied a toilet and small basin, as well as heating and ventilation systems. The inclusion of these facilities was designed to improve health and living conditions, but also meant there was little reason for prisoners to leave the cell and mix with other prisoners, which was the basic principle of the separate system.

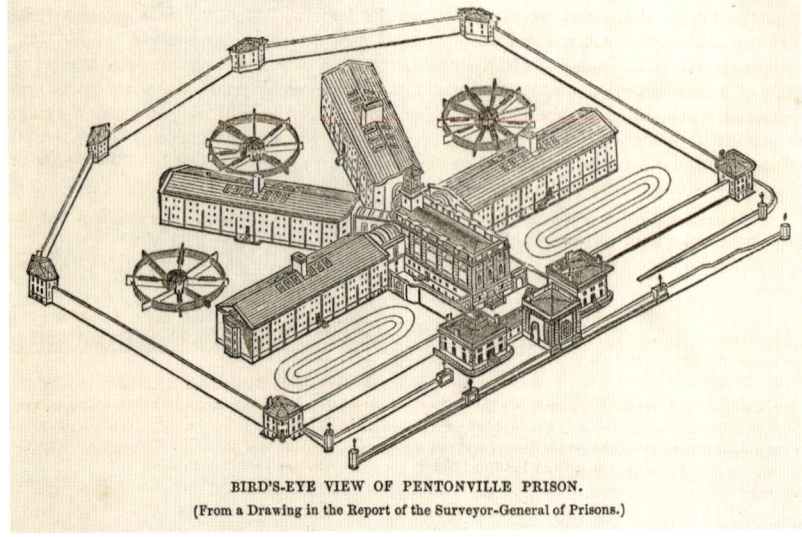

▲ A plan of Pentonville Prison

The separate system

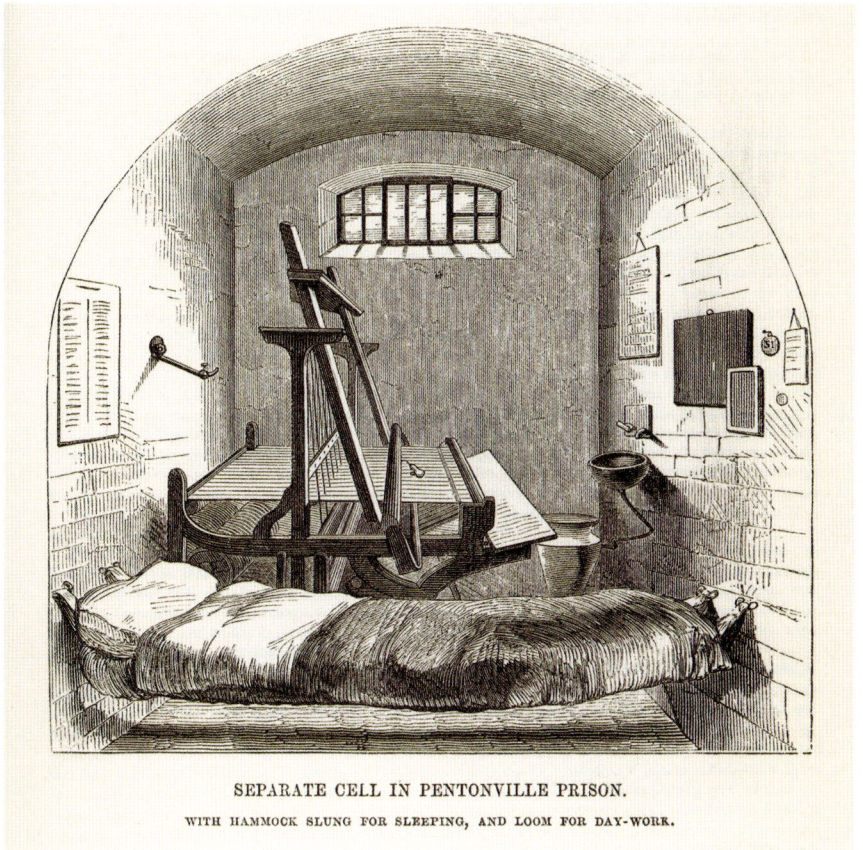

SEPARATE CELL IN PENTONVILLE PRISON.
WITH HAMMOCK SLUNG FOR SLEEPING, AND LOOM FOR DAY-WORK.

▲ A cell in Pentonville, with a hammock for sleeping and a weaving loom for the prisoner to work on. Prisoners were put to useful work to show that hard work and effort could make them productive citizens. It was hoped that once released they would seek honest employment rather than returning to crime

The separate system was designed to isolate prisoners, allowing time for them to reflect on their crimes and avoid being a bad influence on each other. Prison walls were thick to limit communication between cells and the cell layout was designed for prisoners to spend long periods in isolation without there being a negative impact on their health. Cells had hammock-style beds with mattresses and blankets that could be folded away to create more work space during the day.

Prisoners were expected to work. Work was deliberately boring and repetitive. Weaving looms were installed into some cells to ensure inmates could work without leaving their room, while others engaged in oakum picking – the unravelling and cleaning of old rope.

Prisoners were allowed out of their cells for a short period of time to exercise or to visit the chapel, but even on these occasions they were prevented from seeing or speaking with other inmates.

The impact of Pentonville

More than 50 prisons were built based on the design of Pentonville. Some historians consider it a significant development in the history of prisons because of its innovative design and because it was undoubtedly cleaner and better run than other prisons.

However, crime rates were not significantly reduced by Pentonville and the other new prisons which had adopted a similar model. This led some people at the time to believe prisons were not enough of a deterrent. There were other criticisms of Pentonville too. Many complained that such prisons were expensive to run and so cost the public too much money. Some people complained that inmates were subjected to repetitive work rather than an education which could improve their lives outside of prison. There were also concerns that the separate system caused poor mental health among the isolated prisoners. This concern was supported by high rates of suicide.

'Hard labour, hard fare and hard board'

Elizabeth Fry voiced her concern about the separate system in a letter to the government in 1841 (before the building of Pentonville). She criticised the government for being overly concerned with retribution and deterrence, rather than reforming the moral character of prisoners so that they might move away from crime and have a better life on their release from prison. She was also worried about the impact isolation had on the mind and body. She believed inmates needed to see something beyond just the prison walls.

However, her views did not mirror those of the government at the time. The introduction of the 1865 Prisons Act made conditions at Pentonville and other prisons around the country significantly harsher to increase the deterrent effect of prisons. This Act enforced a strict and uniform regime of punishment in all prisons across Britain. It did not aim to reform inmates through education, religion or work and was seen by many prison reformers as a step backwards from the recommendations of Howard and Fry.

Sir Edmund Du Cane, who was Assistant Director of Prisons, declared that prisoners could expect 'Hard labour, hard fare (diet) and hard board (accommodation)':

- **Hard labour:** Prisoners would be subjected to physically demanding work for up to 8 hours per day. This included pointless work such as turning the crank, a handle that had to be turned up to 20 times per minute and could be made more demanding by prison guards who might tighten the crank to make it harder to turn. Prisoners might also walk on a treadwheel. They would be permitted a 5-minute rest break for every 10 minutes walked and could walk up to 5000 metres in a day.

- **Hard fare:** Prisoners would be given a bland and boring diet. This usually involved the same food being served on the same day.
- **Hard board:** Hammocks and mattresses were replaced with hard wooden board beds.

This harsher prison is referred to as 'the silent system' (an old concept) because in addition to the changes to work, diet and sleep, prisoners were expected to be silent at all times.

Connect & Engage

Where can you see evidence of the separate system at work in this photograph?

◀ Prisoners walking on a row of treadwheels at Pentonville Prison in 1895

3.6 Case study 2: The reforms of Robert Peel

Research & Record

Why was the work of Robert Peel so significant?
Complete a copy of the table below using the information on this page and on page 71 to explain the importance of Robert Peel in changes to crime and punishment in this period.

Think carefully about the language you use to state how important each reason was. In column 2, choose a word or phrase from the scale on the right to show the level of importance. Do not fill in column 3 if you think a reason had no or only minimal impact.

Essential	No change could have happened without it
Important	Without it change might have been less widespread or significant
Minimal	Had only a little impact
No importance	No influence at all

Reason	Importance	Explanation
The end of the Bloody Code		
Prison reform		
The Metropolitan Police		

The political career of Robert Peel

Robert Peel was one of the most high-profile politicians of the nineteenth century. He held a number of government positions and became Home Secretary in 1822. It was during this period that Peel made some important contributions to penal reform.

Peel had many strengths as a politician:

- He was open to new ideas, as evidenced by his work on penal reform which considered many of Elizabeth Fry's suggestions.
- He was able to see bills through parliament because he was confident in managing the concerns and reactions of other MPs.
- He used his positions of influence as Home Secretary and then Prime Minister (1834–35 and again 1841–46) to implement change. These positions meant that he had powers to guide new laws through parliament, create or abolish crimes and set or change the punishment of them.

▲ A portrait of Robert Peel

Contribution to penal reform

As Home Secretary Robert Peel was responsible for law and order. He still needed to persuade parliament before changes to law could be made, but he was able to influence a number of significant changes during the 1820s.

The end of the Bloody Code

We have already seen that the Bloody Code was problematic and did not provide the deterrent that law makers had intended it to, for several reasons. Peel wanted to change attitudes to punishment and favoured criminal reform and crime prevention over shock deterrence methods such as the Bloody Code.

Peel still believed in retribution, but he advocated for punishments that were proportionate to the crime committed. He reduced the number of crimes punishable by death to 100 (remember, it had been 225!), removing many minor and social crimes from the list. His actions effectively brought the Bloody Code to an end, leaving only the most violent crimes subject to the death penalty.

Prison reform

Peel persuaded parliament to pass the 1823 Gaols Act. While he was influenced by the findings of campaigners such as Elizabeth Fry, Peel also wanted to build a system of punishment that was both organised and logical. He believed it was important that the same crime was consistently punished in the same way. The law aimed to improve conditions for prisoners so that prisons could become effective places of reform. It stated that:

- prison wardens should be paid a wage so that they did not need to exploit prisoners or be influenced by them
- female wardens should be employed to oversee female prisoners
- prisoners were not to be held in chains or irons (metal chains or bands around a prisoner's hands and/or feet to prevent them moving)
- prison chaplains (men of the Church) should make regular visits to prisons.

The new measures had a positive effect, but there was still some way to go and it took time for Peel's reforms to be introduced. It was not until the 1853 Prison Act that prison inspections became compulsory.

The development of the Metropolitan Police Force

As you have already learned (see pages 60–61), crime rates had risen dramatically in the early nineteenth century and the government acknowledged the need for a more centralised, formal police force. However, the public were resistant to this due to the cost to taxpayers and concerns a new police force would affect their freedoms.

Peel was sympathetic to public and press concern. To build confidence in his new police force, he established a code of conduct, which still provides the foundations for modern-day policing.

Connect & Engage

How significant was the work of Robert Peel?

1 Explain how Robert Peel's attitude to punishment influenced his work.
2 Identify the change that you think is the most significant of all Peel's work. Explain why this change is significant, thinking about its impact and what makes it more significant than his other work.

- Police officers would use force only when necessary. They would be armed with just a baton.
- Police officers would wear a civilian- rather than military-style uniform. This would make them easily identifiable.
- As a professional force officers, would receive training and be paid a wage for their work.
- Police officers would be completely impartial and treat everyone fairly and equally.

> **Exam Tip**
>
> **Question 4: Explain why …**
> Your exam will have a question that asks you to explain why change took place. Think before you write using the 3Ds: **decode**, **decide** and **develop**.
>
> **Decode** the question and work out the focus of the question.
>
> Staying focused on the question is crucial. Including information that is not relevant or writing about the wrong topic wastes time and gains no marks. Here's how to 'decode' a question.
>
> **What are the command words?**
> The question starts 'Explain why'. You need to explain at least one reason.
>
> **What is the content focus?**
> Focus on the developments in law enforcement. You need to include at least three aspects of supporting knowledge throughout your answer.
>
> Explain why there were developments in law enforcement in the years c1700–c1900.
> You may use the following in your answer:
> - The hue and dry
> - The Bow Street Runners
>
> You **must** also use information of your own. (12 marks)
>
> **What is the conceptual focus?**
> The historical concept is causation. Describing methods of law enforcement is not enough to get the higher-level marks. Focus on explaining why there were developments in law enforcement and then support with examples from your knowledge.
>
> **How many marks are available?**
> '12 marks' indicates you should spend about 18 minutes on the question and write no more than three paragraphs (one per aspect of supporting knowledge).
>
> **Decide** how to organise your answer before you start to write.
>
> You do not have the time to tell the story of all the law enforcement methods throughout the period. The focus is on the developments in law enforcement and why these changes occurred. Decide the main reasons you want to explain and then organise these reasons into three paragraphs. One possible approach is:
>
> Paragraph 1: Reason 1: changes in society – explain that community methods of policing such as the hue and cry and town watchmen were no longer adequate for growing towns and cities.
>
> Paragraph 2: Reason 2: individuals – explain how John and Henry Fielding developed the Bow Street Runners to address the changing needs of law enforcement.
>
> Paragraph 3: Reason 3: individual – explain how Robert Peel influenced the 1829 Metropolitan Police Act and how this addressed the changing needs of law enforcement, including the limitations of the Bow Street Runners.
>
> **Develop** your answer – make sure you explain and support the points you make.
>
> Do not simply state that growing towns and cities put pressure on the existing approach to law enforcement – explain how and give specific examples. Do not simply state that the Fielding brothers addressed this problem by setting up the Bow Street Runners. Explain why this was important and how it changed law enforcement.

Apply ▶ Exam Practice

Question 4 style

Explain why there were changes to the definitions of crime in years c1500–c1900.
You may use the following in your answer:
- Guy Fawkes
- Highway robbery

You **must** also use information of your own. (12 marks)

3.7 Eighteenth- and nineteenth-century Britain review

Review

What led to changes in crime and punishment during the eighteenth and nineteenth centuries?

Copy and complete the table below to review the period. Use the cards on page 75 to guide you.

Theme	Developments in the eighteenth and nineteenth centuries	Key individuals	Other factors
Definitions of crime	Evidence of both change and continuity: • Religious tensions eased, therefore witchcraft and heresy were no longer a concern. • Society changed because of rapid population growth and urbanisation because of the Industrial Revolution. • The government feared mass rebellion and this influenced cases such as the Tolpuddle Martyrs. • Crimes such as theft, smuggling and poaching continued into the eighteenth century. • Changes to how these crimes were committed (e.g. highway robbery, was sometimes violent) and frequency (e.g. smuggling became more of a problem) were a concern.		
Attitudes towards punishment	Significant changes in the nineteenth century: • Deterrence continued to be a priority, but people began to question its effectiveness. • The Bloody Code came to an end. • Public executions ended, but hangings continued in private. • Transportation ended because prisons were being used more widely instead. • By the mid-nineteenth century, prisons became the most common form of punishment. • Some people favoured prevention and reform over harsh acts of deterrence.		

Theme	Developments in the eighteenth and nineteenth centuries	Key individuals	Other factors
Methods of law enforcement	Reached a turning point: • Existing methods of law enforcement such as parish constables and town watchmen were becoming ineffective as towns and cities grew. • The Bow Street Runners. • There was a move towards centralised rather than local policing. • The first professional police force in England is established. • It became compulsory for every region to set up a professional police force. • The CID – the emphasis was on detection rather than prevention.		

Individuals
- John and Henry Fielding
- Robert Peel
- John Howard
- Elizabeth Fry

Government/authorities
- Import duties
- 1773 Waltham Black Act
- The Bloody Code and penal reform
- 1823 Gaols Act
- 1829 Metropolitan Police Act
- 1856 Prisons Act
- 1856 Police Act

Attitudes in society
- Protest and rioting because of economic downturn and increased poverty
- Trade unionism
- Deterrence and retribution

Science and technology
- The Royal Society
- Photography

Apply ▶ Recall Challenges

1 Sequencing

Sort these ten events from all three periods you have studied so far into chronological order:

Bow Street Runners	End of trial by ordeal
Tolpuddle Martyrs	Introduction of transportation
Forest Laws	Gaols Act
Metropolitan Police Act	CID established
Gunpowder Plot	Pentonville Prison

2 Know the key individuals

Look at these key individuals:

- Henry Fielding
- John Howard
- Elizabeth Fry
- Robert Peel

What contributions did they make to developments in punishment/law enforcement?
What impact did they have?

3.8 Eighteenth- and nineteenth-century Britain exam practice

Apply ▶ Exam Practice

Revisiting Question 3: Comparison

Explain **one** way in which the nature of law enforcement in medieval England was different from the nature of law enforcement in the eighteenth and nineteenth centuries. (4 marks)

Exam Tip

Question 3: Comparison (difference)

Look again at the advice on how to approach this type of question on page 37.

This question compares **one feature** (the nature of law enforcement) in two different time periods.
Focus on **difference**. Do not write about similarities.
When you compare the feature the nature of law enforcement in different periods, you need to support with **an example from both time periods**. Think about: • the role of the local communities • the work of the Fielding brothers.

Apply ▶ Exam Practice

Revisiting Question 3: Comparison

Explain **one** way in which methods of policing in early modern England were different from methods of policing in the nineteenth century. (4 marks)

Exam Tip

Question 3: Comparison (difference)

Look again at the advice on page 37 before answering this question 3.

Remember to focus on explaining a **difference** and supporting with **an example from both time periods**.

Think about:
- the importance of communities for overseeing policing in early modern England
- how this had developed into a centralised system of policing by the mid-nineteenth century.

Apply ▶ Exam Practice

Revisiting Question 4: Change or continuity

Explain why there were changing attitudes to punishment in the years 1700–1900. (12 marks)

You may use the following in your answer:
- The Bloody Code
- Pentonville Prison.

You **must** also use information of your own.

Exam Tip

Question 4: Explaining change or continuity

Look again at the advice on how to approach this type of question on page 73.

Remember to use the 3Ds:

- **Decode** the question (work out the focus of the question).
- **Decide** how to organise your answer into paragraphs.
- **Develop** your answer by explaining and supporting the points you make. Explain why attitudes to punishment changed between 1700 and 1900. Support each reason with specific knowledge.

Make sure you have included three aspects of knowledge across your whole answer.

Use connectives to tie what you know to the question.

Apply ▶ Exam Practice

Revising Question 5/6: Judgement question

'The work of Elizabeth Fry was the most important development in punishment in the years c1700 to c1900.'

How far do you agree? Explain your answer. (16 marks)

You may use the following in your answer:

- 1823 Gaols Act
- the end of the Bloody Code.

You **must** also use information of your own.

Exam Tip

Question 5/6: Judgement question

Remember the 3Ds:

- **Decode** the question.
- **Decide** how to organise your answer into paragraphs.
- **Develop** your explanation of why you agree and disagree that the work of Elizabeth Fry was the most important development in punishment.

Support each argument with specific knowledge. Make sure you have included three aspects of knowledge across your whole answer.

Remember, you must reach a **judgement** about how far you agree with the statement. The easiest way to do this is to write a conclusion at the end of your answer. For example, when answering this question:

- Decide whether you agree or disagree that the work of Elizabeth Fry was the most important development in punishment and begin your paragraph with *'In conclusion, the work of Elizabeth Fry was / was not the most important development in punishment because …'*
- Go on to explain why you have reached this judgement by explaining the importance of Fry's work and other significant developments of relevance, such as the role of Robert Peel.

Part 4 c1900–present: Crime and punishment in modern Britain

▲ Anti-death penalty protester Violet Van der Elst

Connect and Engage – Violet Van der Elst

By the 1950s, a debate about the use of the death penalty was raging in British society. Protests outside of prisons holding executions were becoming commonplace and a series of controversial cases, including those of Ruth Ellis and Derek Bentley, had sparked media action.

It came as little surprise to the police in July 1955 to see the face of Violet Van der Elst when they arrived at Holloway Prison to deal with protestors calling for the fate of Ruth Ellis to be overturned. Violet had attended most executions in the last 30 years and was a vigorous campaigner against the use of capital punishment.

A slow-moving anti-capital punishment movement had been on the rise since the late nineteenth century. Changes in society and the use of prison as an effective alternative punishment had raised serious questions about the use of the death penalty in the twentieth century. From 1934, Violet dedicated her time and money to campaigning for an end to executions. She was passionate, eccentric and, at times, controversial. She had a reputation for leading loud and disruptive protests, usually arriving in her Rolls-Royce, equipped with loudspeakers and posters. She was frequently sanctioned by police for breaching the peace and was arrested on several occasions.

There was a sudden surge in support for the death penalty after the Second World War as people considered the hanging of Nazi war criminals a justified action. Britain's famous executioner Albert Pierrepoint was sent to Germany to help carry out the sentences.

However, Violet Van der Elst remained stubborn in her protests and it wasn't long before the media were captivated by her methods. She divided public opinion: to some she was a loud nuisance, whereas others compared her influence to that of Elizabeth Fry or suffragette campaigner Emmeline Pankhurst.

In Britain, capital punishment was finally ended in 1965. Violet passed away six months later, having witnessed the change she had campaigned so long for.

Connect & Engage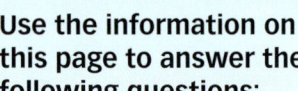

Use the information on this page to answer the following questions:

1. Explain what is meant by the term 'anti-capital punishment movement'.
2. Why do you think the surge in popularity of the death penalty after the Second World War didn't last?
3. What can the work of Violet Van der Elst tell us about changing attitudes to punishment in the twentieth century?

4.1 The nature and changing definitions of criminal activity

> **Research & Record**
>
> 'Technology has had the biggest impact on changing definitions of old crimes.'
>
> 1. How far do you agree with this statement? As you read through pages 79–81, complete a copy of the table below to demonstrate evidence for and against the statement. Think about the crimes of theft, smuggling and terrorism.
>
> | Agree | Disagree |
> |---|---|
> | | |
> | | |
>
> 2. Then, evaluate the impact that technology has had on definitions of old crimes. Choose the appropriate phrase from the scale below and explain why you have come to this conclusion.
>
>   A total change — Significant change — Some changes but mainly continuity — Considerable continuity — No change
>
> 3. Choose the strongest piece of evidence to support your overall conclusion.

From 1900 onwards, there was significant change in British society which influenced definitions of crime and the nature of law enforcement and punishment.

After the Second World War, Britain became a more multi-ethnic society. Many people from Commonwealth countries (former colonies of the British Empire) moved to Britain. As Britain became more ethnically, racially and religiously diverse, this led to new definitions of crime, such as **race crime**, and, in more recent times, questions about the way police deal with racially motivated crimes.

A new age of science and technology

The twentieth century also became an age of developed science and technology. Scientific thinking had already led to great developments in other fields, such as medicine. But it had had a limited impact on crime and punishment until the twentieth when it allowed for easier detection of criminal activity and, along with advances in technology, led to some major developments in policing.

However, in addition to helping policing, technology affected crime. It has led to new definitions of crime, such as hacking, and it has also assisted criminals to find new ways to conduct old crimes, such as identity theft.

The continuity and change in nature of old crimes

Theft

Identity theft has become a big concern in the twenty-first century. Scammers trick people into handing over personal information about themselves such as bank details and passwords. This kind of crime has been made much easier with the development of the internet and fraudsters often use computers or mobile devices to access accounts, send messages and make scam phone calls. The internet has also aided criminals with copyright theft in which people illegally copy films, television programmes and music without paying for them.

However, developments in technology have not stopped traditional methods of theft in which a person steals goods. What has changed are the goods that are targeted. Technological goods such as cars and mobile devices have become attractive to thieves because of their high value. Car theft has become one of the largest categories of crime in Britain today.

Smuggling

Smuggling first became an issue in the early modern period and posed significant challenges to the authorities during the eighteenth century. Smuggling has continued into the modern period, but the items that are smuggled have changed as transport has enabled greater movement.

Smugglers still bring in goods such as alcohol and tobacco, often from continental Europe where they can be purchased at cheaper prices and without UK tax duties. These are then sold illegally in Britain for profit. Illegal drugs are also smuggled into modern Britain. Police try to tackle smuggling with the use of sniffer dogs, x-rays and scanners, which are used at ports and airports across the UK. Drug smugglers can be sent to prison if they are caught.

In the modern period, smugglers also bring people into the country. This type of smuggling can be put divided two categories:

- People smuggling: Some people pay smugglers to bring them across borders to enter Britain illegally. Often, they are escaping war or violence in their own countries. People smugglers can be sent to prison if they are caught.
- Human trafficking: Some people are brought into Britain against their will or are deceived into coming with false promises of work. The victims are usually forced into prostitution or enslavement. Traffickers can be sent to prison if they are caught.

Smuggling was seen as a social crime during earlier periods and many people today still take a light view of the illegal import of alcohol and cigarettes. These types of smuggling are still categorised as crimes against authority due to the avoidance of import tax. But the public are much less tolerant of the smuggling of illegal drugs and people, which are viewed as very serious crimes by both the public and the authorities. In addition to being crimes against authority, both of these crimes can have serious consequences for the people involved and for this reason are also considered to be crimes against the person.

Terrorism

Throughout history there are examples of people using violence to gain supporters who are sympathetic to their views or cause. For example, William I experienced several serious rebellions by Anglo-Saxons which threatened Norman authority. Similarly, Guy Fawkes and his co-conspirators challenged the authority of James I with a plot to blow up parliament.

Today, these acts would probably be classed as terrorism. Terrorism is the use of violence, fear and intimidation to publicise a political, racial, ideological or religious cause. There has been an increase in the number of terrorist attacks during the last 200 years because weapons and communications have become more sophisticated. The government takes terrorism very seriously and those who are found guilty of committing acts of terror can face life imprisonment. There is also wide public condemnation for acts of terrorism, because society as a whole is less violent than in previous time periods, and because terrorists target innocent people who have no direct influence over government policies.

Throughout the twentieth century various terrorist organisations operated in the UK. From the 1970s the IRA (Irish Republican Army) used violence to campaign for Irish independence from Britain.

On 7 July 2005, extremist terrorists carried out attacks in London. Bombs were detonated on public transport, including the London Underground and a bus. Fifty-two people were killed and nearly eight hundred more were injured.

▲ Tributes left at Kings Cross Tube station four days after the London bombings, July 2005

4.2 New definitions of crime

Research & Record

How has the nature of crime changed during the modern period?

Use pages 82–84 to complete a copy of this table. Write a description for the nature of each crime. You should include:

- theft
- smuggling and human trafficking
- terrorism
- race crime
- hate crime
- domestic violence
- driving offences
- drug crime.

The nature of crime	Crime and description
Crimes against authority	
Crimes against the person	
Crimes against property	

Race crimes

By the 1960s, nearly one million **migrants** had settled in the UK from Commonwealth countries such as Jamaica, India and Pakistan. As a result of public prejudice, new laws were needed to ensure that people could not be treated unfairly because of their race or ethnic background.

In 1968, the Race Relations Act made it illegal to refuse housing, employment or public services to anyone on the basis of their race, ethnicity or national origins. In 1976, an amendment to the law gave individuals the right to take claims of discrimination to the civil court.

The response by some members of the public to increasing immigration throughout the twentieth and twenty-first centuries has led to expanding definitions of hate crime. In 2006, the Racial and Religious Hatred Act criminalised any attempts to cause hatred based on an individual's race or religion.

Murder of Stephen Lawrence

Stephen Lawrence was a black British teenager from south-east London. His parents, Neville and Doreen Lawrence, had moved to the UK from Jamaica during the 1960s. He was studying for his A levels and planned to become an architect.

On 22 April 1993, Stephen was murdered by a gang of white men in a racially motivated attack while he was waiting at a bus stop. The investigation into Stephen's murder sparked concerns about the way in which the police dealt with race crimes. They were criticised for not acting quickly enough on evidence, which made it difficult to convict those responsible for Stephen's murder. Many people believed that the police treated this case differently because the victim was black.

It took years of constant campaigning before Stephen's family got any justice for his murder. The initial court case was dropped due to lack of evidence, but, in 2012, two of the original suspects were found guilty of his murder after new evidence was found. No further action has been taken against the other suspects.

▲ The Metropolitan Police released this image of Stephen Lawrence, left, and his brother Stuart

An investigation into the Metropolitan Police in 1999 concluded that internal racism in the force had been a factor in the failure to investigate Stephen's murder thoroughly. In 2021, an independent review into police behaviour was conducted. The final review of the 'Casey report' found that racism and other forms of discrimination were still an issue in the police force.

As a result, the London Policing Board (an independent body) was set up to oversee the improvements recommended in the Casey report. Stuart Lawrence, Stephen's brother, joined the board in September 2023.

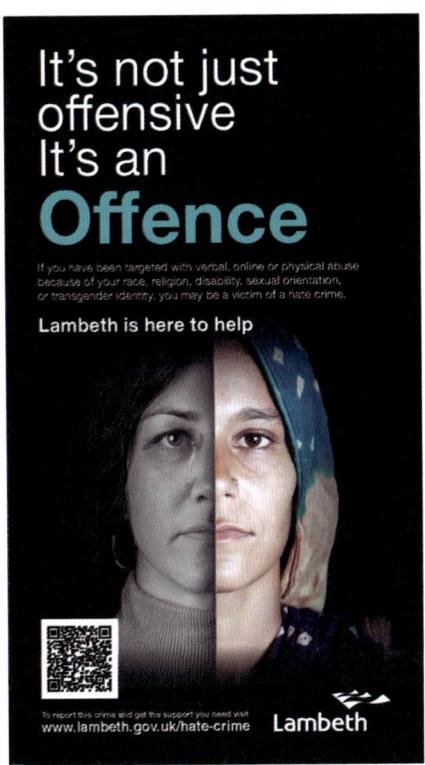

▲ A hate crime poster

Hate crime

In the second half of the twentieth century and into the twenty-first century, new laws have been implemented that mean a person can be prosecuted in court for a hate crime. These include offences which have been committed because of someone's race, religion, disability, gender, sexual orientation or transgender identity.

Domestic violence

In the nineteenth century relationships were seen as a private matter and, as a result, the authorities turned a blind eye to any violent or abusive behaviour. Men could be accused and punished for murdering their wives, but few other cases of domestic violence were ever prosecuted.

The twentieth century saw changes in attitudes towards women. The campaign for women's votes, their contribution to the First and Second World Wars and a campaign for equal rights during the 1960s all influenced the way in which society viewed women.

Since the 1970s laws have been passed to protect people in violent or abusive relationships. These laws protect everyone, regardless of gender or sexuality:

- The Domestic Violence Act was passed in 1976. This allowed an individual to seek legal protection from a violent partner.
- In 1991, rape within marriage became a crime.
- In 2014, the law changed again to include controlling and coercive behaviour. This includes controlling who a person can see, what they can wear and preventing access to money.

Driving offences

During the nineteenth century it became a crime to drive a horse-drawn coach while drunk. With the invention of the motor car in 1885 and mass production throughout the twentieth century, cars became cheaper and driving grew in popularity. It became illegal to drive a car while drunk in 1925 and, in 1967, a new law set a maximum limit of alcohol a person could have in their bloodstream to drive legally. Today drink-driving is widely condemned, but it took a while for new laws to be accepted. Throughout the 1970s, it was considered quite normal to drive after a few alcoholic drinks, but an effective government campaign helped spread awareness of its dangers and played a big role in changing attitudes.

Advertising campaigns have also highlighted the dangers of speeding and drivers who are caught breaking the speed limit can be fined and even lose their licence for repeat offending. In response to changing technology the government introduced new laws in 2003 that made it illegal to use a mobile phone while driving.

Drug crimes

The demand for illegal drugs has increased since the 1960s. In response, the government introduced new laws, including the Misuse of Drugs Act which was passed in 1971:

- The law made it illegal to possess, sell or produce drugs.
- Drugs were put into three categories: Class A, Class B and Class C. Class A drugs are considered the most harmful and therefore carry the most severe punishments.

The criminalisation of some drugs is a controversial issue. The authorities can face difficulties in dealing with drug-related crimes because some people view recreational drug use as a social crime. Some argue that using drugs should be a matter of personal choice, while others believe the legalisation of some drugs would help tackle crimes associated with illegal drug dealing, such as gang-related violence and human trafficking.

▲ A rally for the legalisation of cannabis in London, 2014

Apply ▶ Exam Practice

Revisiting Question 3: Comparison

Explain **one** way in which attitudes towards smuggling in the period c1700–c1900 were similar to attitudes towards smuggling in the period c1900 to present.

(4 marks)

Exam Tip

Question 3: Comparison (similarity)

Look again at the advice on how to approach this type of question on page 37.

This question compares **one feature** (attitudes towards smugglers) in two different time periods.
Focus on **similarity**. Do not write about differences.
When you compare the feature of attitudes to smugglers in different periods, you need to support with **an example from both time periods**. Think about: • the nature of smuggling in both time periods • public attitudes to smuggling in both periods and how these remained similar over time.

Revision Tip

It is important that you know the nature (the type) of crime committed and can make judgements about why these definitions might or might not change during each of the time periods you study. This is also important to understanding the bigger picture and identifying change and continuity between time periods.

Apply ▶ Exam Practice

Revisiting Question 4: Explain why

Explain why there were new definitions of crime in the years c1900–present.
You may use the following in your answer:
- drink-driving
- race crime.

(12 marks)

Exam Tip

Support your answer with specific knowledge

Make sure you support your answer with specific knowledge of the topic. For example:

> There were new definitions of crime in the years c1900– present because during this time Britain became a more multicultural society. By the 1960s, nearly one million people had migrated to Britain from Commonwealth countries. This led to the creation of new laws such as the Race Relations Act, which meant that people from countries such as India, Pakistan and Jamaica could not be refused employment, housing or public services because of their race or ethnicity. Increasing migration throughout the twentieth and twenty-first centuries has led to …

The first sentence makes the argument clear – a reason for new definitions of crime in the modern period.

Precise knowledge is being used to support the argument and prove the reason is correct. This paragraph should be completed with more supporting knowledge which should be linked back to the question.

4.3 The nature of law enforcement c1900–present

Research & Record

How has the role of the local communities in law enforcement changed over time?

Use information on this page to complete your own copy of this table. Add your own examples.

The role of the local communities c1900–present day	The role of the local communities before 1900
Reporting crime to the police	Participating in the hue and cry to apprehend the criminal

The role of local communities

Today, the police have a responsibility to keep people safe. Most people rely on the police to detect crime, but to encourage greater community engagement, various measures have been taken to ensure crimes are reported to the police.

During the 1980s, after an increase in crime, the **Neighbourhood Watch** scheme was introduced. The system is voluntary but encourages residents to work together to tackle crime by keeping an eye on each other's property. This initiative is focused on measures for preventing crime, so groups might meet to discuss issues in the local area and can pass on information to the police to help keep their local area safe.

People are not expected to apprehend criminals, but they are encouraged to report crime or suspicious behaviour to the police. Usually, this can be done by phoning or texting special tip lines. In 2016, the British Transport Police launched the 'See it, Say it, Sorted' campaign to encourage passengers to keep themselves and others safe by reporting suspicious behaviour on trains or at stations. The campaign is promoted nationwide with posters and voice announcements.

▲ A 'See it, Say it, Sorted' poster on the London Underground

Apply ▶ Exam Practice

Revisiting Question 3: Comparison question

Explain **one** way in which the role of the local communities in law enforcement in the years c1000 to c1500 was different from the role of the local communities in law enforcement in the years c1900 to present. *(4 marks)*

> **Exam Tip**
>
> Look again at the advice on how to approach this type of question on page 37.
>
> Remember to focus on explaining a difference between the time periods.
>
> - Consider the responsibilities of the local community in the period c1000 to c1500 and how they were expected to apprehend criminals, provide evidence and oversee justice.
> - Consider the responsibilities of the local community in the period c1900 to present and how schemes and campaigns encourage an active role in reporting crime for the authorities to deal with.
>
> | |
> |---|
> | This question compares **one feature** (i.e. the role of the local community in law enforcement) in two different time periods. |
> | Focus on **difference**. Do not go into similarities. |
> | When you compare the role of the local communities in law enforcement in different periods, you need to support with an example from both time periods. |

Developments in policing since 1900

> **Research & Record**
>
> **Detection, prevention and solving crime: How did the work of the police change from 1900?**
>
> Use pages 87–89 to complete a copy of this table. Categorise information to show how the work of the police has developed from c1900–present to find new ways of detecting crime, preventing crime and solving crime.
>
> Detecting crime = How do the police know a crime has been committed?
>
> Preventing crime = How do the police actively deter criminals from committing crime?
>
> Solving crime = How do the police collect and use evidence to solve crime?
>
> | Detecting crime | Preventing crime | Solving crime |
> |---|---|---|
> | | | |

During the twentieth century there were significant changes to methods of policing. Because of this the role of a police officer also changed. At the start of the period there were 200 separate police forces across Britain and they rarely worked together or shared information. Much of a police officer's day was spent walking the beat and they carried a baton and whistle which could be used to call for assistance if needed. However, significant investment in the police throughout the twentieth century led to some important changes:

- In 1947, the Police Training College was established to train new recruits. Rather than starting with very basic training and learning from a more experienced officer on the job, new officers entered the force with knowledge and understanding of their role.
- Developments in science and technology enabled new specialised units to develop, providing new ways to find and convict criminals.

Increased specialisation

The development of specialised units has helped police tackle specific types of crime. Often, such units are set up in response to changes in society and the emergence of new crimes. An example of this is the Metropolitan Police Bomb Squad, which was set up in 1971 in response to an increased number of IRA (Irish Republican Army) terror attacks.

Special units are highly trained to target a specific area of crime. These include drug squads, fraud squads, firearms units, dog-handling units, cyber-crime units and traffic police to deal with driving offences such as speeding and drink driving.

The use of science and technology

Modern policing makes use of science and technology to support crime detection, prevention and solving. These developments have enabled the police to respond more effectively to crime by reaching crime scenes more quickly and gathering a wider range of evidence. The use of fingerprinting and DNA collection for evidence is known as forensic science.

1901

The Metropolitan Police establishes its fingerprint branch. Individuals have their fingerprints taken, which can then be matched to fingerprints at a crime scene. The police keep records on file to form a database which can be shared with other forces. In 1902, the first fingerprint conviction is made. Blood groups are discovered, enabling police officers to match samples from crime scenes with the blood type of the suspect.

1909

Police officers are given bicycles for the first time. This helps them travel more quickly. The first police car is introduced in 1919 but they are not rolled out across the police force for more than a decade.

1930s

Police cars and motorbikes are introduced across the force. They help speed up the response time for officers attending crime scenes. Radios are installed in police cars to improve communication between the station and officers. The 999 emergency telephone number is introduced in 1937.

1960s

Police officers are equipped with personal radios. The first video surveillance is installed at a London train station.

1974

The Police National Computer is used to create a database accessible to all police forces in the UK. This allows for information sharing of wanted suspects, fingerprint records, stolen or suspect motor vehicles and missing persons.

1980s

DNA evidence is used to identify criminals. It has become the most reliable form of evidence in positive identification.

Preventing crime

As well as helping police officers respond to crime, some of these technological advances have supported the prevention of crime. Recent examples include technology such as CCTV and speed cameras. These act as a deterrent in addition to providing visual evidence of crimes because people can see them before they commit a crime and know that police officers will have a record of their actions. They also show that the area is being monitored for crime.

In 2002, Police Community Support Officers (PCSOs) were introduced as another type of visible deterrent to criminals. They do not have the same level of authority as police officers, but they patrol the streets and their presence offers reassurance to the public.

▲ A police officer uses a police phone box on a London street. These phone boxes could be used to call for back-up or for members of the public to report crimes to the police

Connect & Engage

What evidence of change and continuity for a police officer walking the beat can be seen in this photograph?

Explain your answer using evidence from the photograph and your own knowledge about officers on the beat.

Summarise

Developments in policing during the twentieth century ensured the police were never **SECOND** best when it came to catching criminals:

S = **Speed** of response time greatly improved by better transport.

E = **Evidence** from fingerprinting and blood groups made it easier to link criminals to crime.

C = **Communication** improved greatly between the public and the police with the introduction of the 999 emergency number.

O = **Officers** could communicate with one another better with radio technology.

N = **National database** helped the sharing of information about crime and criminals across the country.

D = **DNA** evidence has become the most effective way of proving a person's involvement in crime.

4.4 Punishment c1900–present

Research & Record

How has the nature of punishment changed in the modern period?
Read pages 90–95 and complete your own copy of this table.

Punishment	Description of changes in the modern period
Prison system	
Non-custodial alternatives	
Treatment of young offenders	
Capital punishment	

During the twentieth and twenty-first centuries there have been changes to the nature and purpose of punishment:

- Prisons focus on the rehabilitation of the criminal.
- There is a range of **non-custodial alternatives** which offer criminals a chance to stay out of prison.

Changes to prisons

Prisons have continued to be the most common form of punishment for serious crimes throughout the modern period. During the nineteenth century, the ambitions of Robert Peel and reformers like Fry and Howard to focus on criminals' reform were set back by the harsh conditions imposed in the 1860s which shifted the focus of prisons from reform to deterrence. However, in the twentieth century, significant changes occurred as prisons became more concerned with the physical and mental well-being of prisoners.

This change is mostly due to attitudes in society. Public attitudes in the twentieth century were far less tolerant of inflicting pain on prisoners, and there was little evidence that harsh treatment of prisoners did anything to reduce crime. Instead, people began to focus on the factors that led to crime, such as poverty. As a result, prisons changed to focus on education and rehabilitation as a means of offenders building a better life for themselves outside once their sentence was complete. There were several developments throughout the twentieth century that enabled this:

- In 1907, the probation system was introduced. On probation, prisoners are released from prison but must comply with certain rules (set depending on their crime) and meet regularly with their probation officer. Failure to do so can result in a return to prison.
- In 1922, the separate system ended. This meant that solitary confinement was no longer used for all offenders. Prisoners were allowed more visits from family, more interaction with other prisoners, and improvements were made to diet and cell conditions. Teachers were employed to provide offenders with a basic education.
- In 1933, the first **open prison** was built. Open prisons allow offenders to move around the prison with more freedom and leave during the day to go to work. They are used for low-risk offenders, and it is hoped these prisoners would leave better prepared for a life within the community. Open prisons continue to operate today.

Today, the government aspires for the prison system to be a place of rehabilitation and reform, rather than simply punishment and deterrence. Prisons are categorised for different types of criminals. This means that people who have committed the most serious crimes are not mixed with people who have committed less serious crimes. Education and training are provided so that inmates can learn a range of knowledge and practical skills inside prison to help them find employment once they are released.

Alternatives to prison

Prisons do not always deal with the social and personal problems that lead a person to crime and if a prisoner is released back into the same environment, they are likely to reoffend. As a result, throughout the twentieth century the government introduced a range of non-custodial alternatives to prison. These help to keep the prison population down and offer some lesser criminals a better chance at rehabilitation. Some alternatives to prison include:

Community service
Some people convicted of minor crimes might be ordered to do unpaid work which benefits the community, such as collecting litter or removing graffiti.

Electronic tagging
Courts can order some criminals to wear an electronic tag. This is usually worn around the ankle and monitors a person's movements. The person is not in prison, but their movements are controlled, usually with a curfew time or a limit on where they can go. Breaking the conditions of an electronic tag can result in the criminal being sent to prison.

▲ An electronic ankle tag

Community Protection Notice (CPN) or Criminal Behaviour Order (CBO)
CPNs and CBOs replaced ASBOs in England and Wales and are court orders that place restrictions on what a person can do, which might include who they can talk to or where they can go. They are used to tackle anti-social behaviour such as vandalism and an offender can be issued with a fine or sent to prison for breaking these rules.

Restorative justice
The criminal meets the victim of their crime (or sometimes a family member) to talk about what they have done and the impact this has had on others. Victims may also have a say in their offender's rehabilitation programme.

Fines
Fines are the most common non-custodial punishment in Britain and require the criminal to pay a sum of money to the state. However, some people may not be able to pay the fine and so may end up in prison for quite a minor offence.

Probation order
Here, the offender lives in the community rather than in prison but under the strict supervision of the probation service. They may be required to attend courses, therapy and/or treatment programmes.

Apply ▶ Exam Practice

Revisiting Question 4: Explain why

Explain why there were changes to the use of prisons in the years c1900–present.

You may use the following in your answer:
- the separate system
- community service. (12 marks)

Exam Tip

Plan your answer

You must include three aspects of content in your answer. Make time to plan what you will include. You may choose to use the bullet points to help develop your answer, or to include different aspects of your own knowledge that are relevant to the question.

Specialised treatment of young offenders

During the eighteenth and nineteenth centuries children were often subject to the same laws and treatment as adults. However, from 1900 attitudes about the treatment of children began to change as a result of government ideas and those of key individuals such as Elizabeth Fry.

Borstals

In 1902, the first borstal opened in Kent for male offenders under the age of 18. Its purpose was to separate young convicts from older criminals.

In 1908, the government passed the Prevention of Crime Act which created a new national system of borstals. Its intention was to emphasise education rather than punishment. Borstals had a structured routine, where **young offenders** took part in work programmes, learned practical skills and had physical exercise each day. However, they were also subject to strict disciplinary regimes and boys could be whipped if they did not stick to them. Many children suffered under these regimes.

Reform in the 1940s

In 1948, the government introduced the Criminal Justice Act which led to changes in the way criminals were punished, including the treatment of young offenders. The act was influenced by Alexander Patterson, who was appointed Commissioner of Prisons in 1922. Patterson spent his career pressing for better treatment of prisoners and believed probation and rehabilitation were essential.

The reforms introduced as part of the 1948 Criminal Justice Act included:

- the introduction of attendance centres for young offenders aged 10–21 – these were non-custodial centres where young people attended daily or weekly sessions which focused on teaching life skills, literacy and numeracy
- the introduction of detention centres – designed as an intervention for young people aged 14 to 20, they housed young criminals for sentences of up to 3 months. They had a more relaxed regime compared to borstals but aimed to deter those housed there from committing further crime
- improvements to the probation service for young people so greater support was given.

▲ A photograph from the 1940s of Feltham Borstal, with some of the boys working in the gardens

Reform in the 1960s

During the 1960s, the law changed again to protect young offenders. The Children and Young Persons Acts of 1963 and 1969 introduced two key developments:

- In 1963, the age of criminal responsibility (the minimum age at which a person is considered to be mature enough to understand their actions and the consequences of breaking the law) was raised from eight to ten years of age.
- In 1969, the law placed a greater emphasis on care orders and supervision by probation officers and social workers rather than prison sentences.

The treatment of young offenders today

In 1982, the government abolished the borstal system and introduced government-run youth detention centres which could house young people for longer sentences. They were introduced to act as a deterrent to try to reduce the levels of youth crime and re-offending, with strict discipline, rules and routines. However, crime and re-offending rates for young people have continued to increase.

▲ A youth detention centre, where the emphasis is on rehabilitation and care for young people

Today there is more emphasis on prevention and care for young people. Youth courts work alongside schools, police, social workers and probation officers to try to prevent young people from falling into a life of crime. Parents can be fined if they do not manage the behaviour of their children and, in some cases, children can be removed from their parents and placed in care.

Offenders under the age of 18 might serve time in a youth offenders institute, which has the same rules as prison. Non-custodial sentences can also be used to monitor the movements and behaviour of a young offender.

Connect & Engage

What evidence can you see in this photograph of changes to the treatment of young offenders over time? Consider how this image demonstrates a different kind of treatment from the way young offenders were treated in earlier time periods and the early part of the twentieth century.

Apply Recall Challenge

How has the treatment of young offenders developed in modern Britain?

Use the information on pages 92–93 to complete your own copy of this bingo card. First, try to answer the questions from memory, then re-read this section to fill in any gaps. Write the answers on the back of your bingo cards. You can use these cards to revise later.

Treatment of young offenders bingo		
What is borstal?	What are youth detention centres?	When was the first borstal opened?
Name two changes in the treatment of young people because of the 1948 Criminal Justice Act.	What did Patterson believe was essential for offenders?	How did the British government establish a national system of borstals?
How were young offenders treated typically before 1900?	Name three key developments in the treatment of young people since 1900.	What was the age of criminal responsibility raised to in 1963?

The abolition of the death penalty

Research & Record

What factors led to the abolition of the death penalty?

Use pages 94–97 to complete your own copy of a table like this. Record details of the role of the government and attitudes in society to show how attitudes towards the death penalty changed throughout the twentieth century.

The role of the government	Attitudes in society

Capital punishment had been a key deterrent throughout the medieval and early modern periods. While its use continued throughout the eighteenth and nineteenth centuries, public reactions to hangings and the failure of the Bloody Code had raised debate about its effectiveness.

By the twentieth century, attitudes were starting to change. The majority of the public and politicians continued to support the use of the death penalty for the most serious crimes, such as murder, but during the 1950s some controversial cases and a greater emphasis on human rights and rehabilitation led to discussions about its **abolition**.

Arguments for the death penalty	Arguments against the death penalty
• It acted as a deterrent. People were concerned that cases of serious crime would increase if criminals no longer faced punishment by hanging. • Execution was cheaper than imprisonment. • There was concern murderers might go on to kill again once they were released. Execution was the only way to ensure they could not. • Execution was the only way to get true justice for the victim's family.	• Other countries had abolished the death penalty and not seen an increase in serious crime. • Prison had become a good alternative punishment. It still removed the criminal from society, which removed the threat of re-offending for the duration of the offender's sentence. • Executions were against religious teachings to forgive and protect the sanctity of life. • Wrongful conviction could result in the execution of an innocent person.

Important cases

Timothy Evans

In 1950, Timothy Evans was executed for the murder of his wife and child. However, it was later discovered that they had been killed by their neighbour, John Christie, who had also murdered others. There was a public outcry that an innocent man had been hanged for a crime he did not commit.

▲ Timothy Evans was wrongly convicted and hanged for killing his family

Derek Bentley

Derek Bentley was hanged for the murder of a police officer in 1953. Bentley had not fired the gun that killed the officer although he was involved in the crime which led to the shooting. However, the person who did shoot the officer was under 18 years of age and therefore could not be executed for the crime. There was deep public sympathy for Bentley, who also had learning disabilities. (See pages 96–97.)

▲ Derek Bentley's execution drew deep public sympathy

Ruth Ellis

Ruth Ellis was the last woman to be hanged in Britain. She was executed in 1955 for the murder of her partner, David Blakely. Blakely had abused her and there was lots of public sympathy for Ellis and what she had suffered. Her case gained a lot of media coverage and there were protests outside Holloway Prison leading up to her execution (as you read on page 78).

▲ Ruth Ellis, the last woman to be hanged in Britain

1908
The Children's Act is introduced which abolishes hanging for under-16s.

1922
The Infanticide Act is passed which abolishes hanging for mothers who kill their newborn babies shortly after birth. This is based on increased understanding that a woman's mental state could be affected by pregnancy and childbirth.

1933
The Young Person's Act ends the hanging of under-18s.

1949
A Royal Commission on capital punishment is set up to consider whether the death penalty for murder in Britain should be changed or abolished. Its report was published in 1953.

1956
The Death Penalty Bill (the first bill to propose full abolition of the death penalty) is passed by the House of Commons but rejected by the House of Lords.

1957
The Homicide Act limits the use of capital punishment to five categories of murder. The Act also takes into account a person's mental state before sentencing.

1965
The Murder Act suspends executions in the UK. The death penalty is abolished for most crimes. No further executions are carried out after this point.

1969
Murder is removed from the list of crimes punishable by death. Execution could still be carried out in extreme circumstances, such as high treason or piracy, but is not used.

1999
The UK adopts the European Convention on Human Rights, formally abolishing the death penalty.

4.5 Case study 1: The Derek Bentley case and its significance for the abolition of the death penalty

Research & Record

How was Derek Bentley's case significant to the abolition of the death penalty?

As you have seen on page 95, Derek Bentley's case was one of the controversial cases during the 1950s that led to discussions in Britain about abolishing the death penalty. Use the information on pages 96–97 to complete your own copy of this quiz card. Write down the answers as you read.

The significance of the Derek Bentley case quiz		
What weapons were Bentley and Craig armed with?	**Where** did the murder of PC Sidney Miles take place?	**When** did the murder of PC Sidney Miles take place?
Name two reactions to the sentencing of Derek Bentley to death.	**Why** was there such public sympathy for Derek Bentley?	**What** is diminished responsibility and when was it introduced into law?
How old was Derek Bentley?	**Which** controversial phrase was used as evidence in court to convict Bentley?	**Why** was Christopher Craig exempt from the death penalty?

The murder of a police constable

During the 1950s Derek Bentley's execution was one of a number of cases which caught public and media attention. Bentley was 19 years of age. He had epilepsy and severe learning disabilities, which made it hard for him to gain employment and to make friends. He was believed to have had a mental age of around ten years.

On 2 November 1952, Bentley and Chistopher Craig, who was 16 years old, were in the process of stealing from a warehouse near London when they were interrupted by police officers Sidney Miles and Frederick Fairfax. Craig had armed himself with a gun and given Bentley a knife and a knuckle duster to carry. PC Fairfax's report stated that when Craig was asked to hand over his gun, Bentley responded with 'Let him have it, Chris'. Craig then opened fire on the police officers, fatally wounding PC Sidney Miles.

▲ PC Sidney Miles was fatally wounded when he interrupted a warehouse robbery

The trial

Both Bentley and Craig were put on trial for murder, a crime which still carried a death sentence in 1952. However, at 16 years of age, Christopher Craig was too young to be sentenced to death. Bentley had not even attempted to use the weapons that were given to him by Craig and his lawyers argued that the words 'Let him have it' had meant for Craig to hand over the gun. Laws at the time meant that Bentley's learning difficulties and mental age were not taken into consideration during his trial.

Both Bentley and Craig were found guilty. Bentley was sentenced to hang and Craig to time in prison.

Reactions to Bentley's sentence

Many people disagreed with Bentley's sentence and there was both public and political pressure to change it to life in prison. Two hundred MPs signed a letter appealing for a change in the sentence and the case gained huge media coverage, thanks in part to Bentley's family, who campaigned vigorously to have his sentence overturned.

The night before Bentley's execution, 5000 protesters gathered outside Wandsworth Prison. But there was no change to Bentley's sentence and he was executed on 28 January 1953.

▲ On 28 January 1953, a large crowd gathered at Wandsworth Prison, London, to learn of the execution of Derek Bentley

The significance of the case

At the time of Bentley's trial English law did not recognise the legal defence of diminished responsibility (when it is argued that a defendant should not be held fully responsible for their actions due to mental impairment), although this had been the subject of legal debate since the eighteenth century and some people had been acquitted of crimes on grounds of insanity. This changed in 1957 when the Homicide Act was introduced. It recognised that a person suffering from a medical or mental condition might not have full ability to exercise self-control or to make rational decisions.

Bentley's case came at a time when debate about the use of the death penalty was increasing. Many people argued that it was a miscarriage of justice and this, alongside other controversial cases, swayed public opinion. Even after the execution, Bentley's family campaigned to clear his name. He was eventually posthumously (after death) pardoned in 1998.

> ### Apply ⏵ Exam Practice
>
> **Revisiting Question 4: Explain why**
>
> Explain why there were changes in attitudes towards the death penalty in the years c1700–present.
>
> You may use the following in your answer:
>
> - the Bloody Code
> - Derek Bentley.
>
> You **must** also use information of your own. (12 marks)

> ### Exam Tip
>
> **Question 4: Explaining change or continuity**
>
> Look again at the advice on how to approach this type of question on page 73.
>
> Remember to use the 3Ds:
>
> - **Decode** the question (work out the focus of the question).
> - **Decide** how to organise your answer into paragraphs.
> - **Develop** your answer by explaining and supporting the points you make. Explain why there were changes in attitudes towards the death penalty c1700 to present. Support each reason with specific knowledge.
>
> Make sure you have included three aspects of knowledge across your whole answer.
>
> Use connectives to tie what you know to the question.

4.6 Case study 2: The treatment of conscientious objectors in the First and Second World Wars

Research & Record

To what extent did attitudes towards conscientious objectors change between the World Wars?

Use pages 98–99 to complete a copy of this table. Record how attitudes and treatment of conscientious objectors changed over the course of the First and Second World Wars. Consider the role of the government and attitudes of society.

	The role of the government	Attitudes of society
First World War		
Second World War		

▲ A 1916 Military Service Act conscription poster

A new war gives rise to a new crime

Britain's military services had traditionally relied on volunteers and when the First World War began in 1914 this was still the case. More than one million men signed up to fight. However, by 1916 there were fewer and fewer volunteers and the government was forced to act to ensure Britain could continue fully with its war efforts.

The Military Service Act was introduced in 1916. It was the first time Britain had used military conscription on this scale. Initially, all unmarried men aged between 18 and 41 were expected to enlist, but later in the year married men were also included. In 1918, the upper age limit was increased to 51.

Some men refused to fight as a matter of conscience. Before conscription this had not been an issue, they would simply not volunteer for service. But now their personal beliefs put them in conflict with the law. These men were called **conscientious objectors**.

Conscientious objectors in the First World War

Types of conscientious objectors

Conscientious objectors, or 'conchies' for short, were treated differently according to how they responded to the call to military duty. Some objected to killing and carrying weapons but were prepared to support the war effort in other ways. They were known as alternativists because they took on alternative jobs such as stretcher bearers or ambulance drivers. As a result, they were treated much more leniently than those who refused to support the war at all.

Absolutists refused to support the war in any way. They were mostly pacifists who were against all forms of violence. They were treated harshly by the government and the public.

Treatment of conscientious objectors

Around 16,000 men requested exemption from military service on grounds of conscience. Tribunals (a type of court) were set up to process claims. They oversaw all claims of exemption, not just those of conscientious objection, but they were notoriously unsympathetic to conchies. Panels often included retired soldiers or those too old to fight but with a clear sense of duty.

If a tribunal refused the exemption and the conscientious objector did not accept the decision, they were punished. Many were imprisoned, usually in solitary confinement to try to weaken their determination. Some were sent to France and given orders to fight on the frontline. If they refused, they were sent to a military court where they could be sentenced to imprisonment – a small number were sentenced to death, but government intervention stopped this.

The treatment of conscientious objectors was deliberately harsh. The government wanted to prevent the spread of pacifism which could threaten Britain's war effort, and it was supported by the media, which portrayed conscientious objectors as cowardly and unpatriotic. The government removed voting rights for conscientious objectors until 1926. The public were also hostile to conchies. Many people had family and friends who had been killed or injured in the war. Conchies became isolated within communities, and many received hate mail or were given white feathers as a symbol of cowardice.

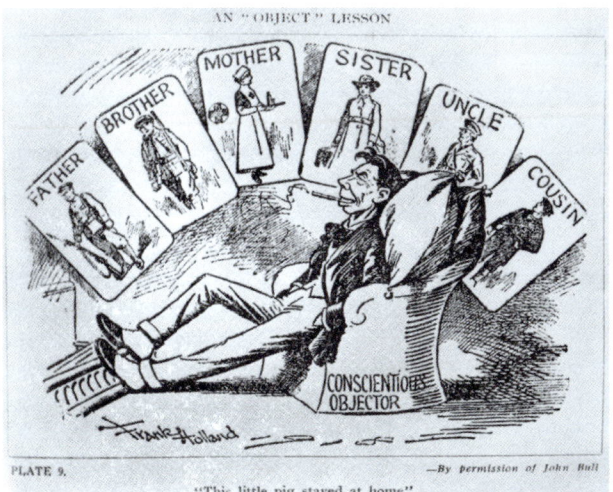

▲ A First World War cartoon showing a conscientious objector at home

Conscientious objectors in the Second World War

During the Second World War, government attitudes towards conscientious objectors changed. Conscription was reintroduced in 1939 and again tribunals dealt with exemption cases. However, they were not allowed to include former soldiers and were less hostile towards conchies. Prison was used as a last resort; instead, conchies were given useful work at home such as farming or jobs in munitions factories.

Public attitudes were less quick to change. Some employers sacked conscientious objectors because they did not agree with their actions. Some conscientious objectors were verbally or physically attacked on the streets.

Summarise

The **CONCHIE** memory aid summarises attitudes and treatment of conscientious objectors during the First and Second World Wars.

C = Conscription was introduced in both the First and Second World Wars

O = Other work was carried out by alternativists who still wanted to help with the war effort

N = No participation in any war-related work from absolutists

C = Conscience put conscientious objectors in direct conflict with the law

H = Hostile attitudes from both society and the government meant conscientious objectors were treated harshly

I = Improved government attitudes between the First World War and the Second World War meant that conscientious objectors were treated less harshly

E = Exemption certificates were needed for conscientious objectors not to participate in both wars

Connect & Engage

Cartoons such as this were commonplace in the media from 1916 until the end of the war in 1918 and had a huge effect on attitudes in society. What evidence can you see of negative attitudes towards conscientious objectors in this source?

4.7 Modern Britain review

Review

What led to changes in crime and punishment during the modern period?

Fill in a table like the one below to review the period. Use the cards at the bottom of the page to guide you.

Theme	Improvements in modern Britain	Role of government	Science and technology	Other factors
Definitions of crime	Evidence of both change and continuity: • Some old crimes continued in new ways, such as smuggling, theft and terrorism. • There were new definitions of crime because of changes in society, such as race crime, domestic violence, driving offences and drug crime. • Conscription in the First World War led to conscientious objection becoming a crime.			
Methods of law enforcement	Significant developments in the twentieth century: • Specialised units were created within the police to deal with certain crimes. • Forensic science, such as fingerprinting and DNA, made a significant impact on policing. • Technological advances allowed police to respond to crime quicker, using cars and the 999 emergency number. • There was improved communication between individual police officers using radio. • Information sharing through a national database allowed police forces nationwide to work together.			
Attitudes towards punishment	Significant changes in the twentieth century: • The prison system changed to focus on rehabilitation. • There were new ideas about the treatment of young offenders. • There was an increase in non-custodial sentences. • The death penalty was abolished.			

Individuals
- Alexander Patterson
- Derek Bentley
- Ruth Ellis
- Timothy Evans

Government/authority
- 1916 Military Service Act
- 1965 Murder Act
- 1968 Race Relations Act
- Race and hate crimes
- Driving offences
- Drug offences
- Prison reform and the introduction of non-custodial sentences

Science and technology
- Fingerprinting
- Blood groups
- DNA
- Transport
- Radios
- Telephones
- Computers

Attitudes in society
- Reaction to conscientious objectors
- Protests at the use of the death penalty
- Changing attitudes to women
- Attitudes to people of different racial, ethnic or religious backgrounds

4.8 Modern Britain exam practice

Apply ▶ Exam Practice

Revisiting Question 3: Comparison question

Explain **one** way in which the treatment of offenders in prisons in the years c1700–c1900 was different from the treatment of offenders in prisons in the years c1900– present. (4 marks)

Exam Tip

Question 3: Comparison (difference)

Look again at the advice on how to approach this type of question on page 37.

Remember to focus on explaining a difference and supporting with an example from both time periods.

- Consider the treatment of prisoners in the period c1700–c1900 such as the separate or silent systems.
- Consider the treatment of prisoners in the period c1900–present and the use of education and rehabilitation.

This question compares **one feature** (i.e. the treatment of offenders in prisons) in two different time periods.
Focus on **difference**. Do not go into similarities.
When you compare the treatment of offenders in prisons in different periods, you need to support with an example from both time periods.

Apply ▶ Exam Practice

Revisiting Question 3: Comparison question

Explain **one** way in which attitudes towards the death penalty in c1500–c1700 were different from attitudes towards the death penalty in c1900–present. (4 marks)

Exam Tip

Comparing time periods (Question 3)

Look again at the advice on how to approach this type of question on page 37.

Remember to focus on explaining a difference and supporting your explanation with an example from both time periods.

- Think about the use of the death penalty as a deterrent in the years c1500–c1700.
- Think about the case of Derek Bentley and changes to the law in the years c1900–present.

Apply — Exam Practice

Revisiting Question 4: Explain why

Explain why developments in science and technology led to improvements in policing in the years c1900–present.

You may use the following in your answer:

- DNA evidence
- police radios.

You **must** also use information of your own.   (12 marks)

Exam Tip

Question 4: Explaining change or continuity

Look again at the advice on how to approach this type of question on page 73.

Remember to use the 3Ds:

- **Decode** the question (work out the focus of the question).
- **Decide** how to organise your answer into paragraphs.
- **Develop** your answer by explaining and supporting the points you make. Explain why developments in science and technology led to improvements in policing c1900 to the present. Support each reason with specific knowledge.

Make sure you have included three aspects of knowledge across your whole answer.

Use connectives to tie what you know to the question.

Apply — Exam Practice

Revisiting Question 4: Explain why

Explain why there were changes to the prison system in the years c1900–present.   (12 marks)

You may use the following in your answer:

- non-custodial sentences
- borstals.

You **must** also use information of your own.

Exam Tip

Explaining why (Question 4)

Look again at the advice on how to approach this type of question on page 73.

Remember to focus on explaining why there were changes, rather than going into detail about what these changes were.

- Think about the aims of punishment in the modern period and how this impacted the prison system.
- Think about different types of offender, such as young people.
- Think about different types of offence, for example, sentences for those committing very serious crimes as opposed to those committing more minor crimes for the first time.

Exam Tip

Question 5/6: Judgement question

Look again at the advice on how to approach this type of question on pages 28–29. Then, answer the questions below.

Remember to:
- **Decode** the question.
- **Decide** how to organise your answer into paragraphs.
- **Develop** your explanation of why you agree or disagree with the statement.

Support each argument with specific knowledge. Make sure you have included three aspects of knowledge across your whole answer. Remember, you need to reach a judgement on the statement in the question.

Apply ▶ Exam Practice

Revising Question 5/6: Judgement question

'Modern-day technology has been the most significant development in the nature of crime in Britain in the years c1900–present.'

How far do you agree? Explain your answer. (16 marks)

You may use the following in your answer:
- computer crime
- conscientious objection.

You **must** also use information of your own.

Apply ▶ Exam Practice

Revising Question 5/6: Judgement question

'The abolition of the death penalty was a turning point in attitudes to punishment in the years c1900–present.'

How far do you agree? Explain your answer. (16 marks)

You may use the following in your answer:
- Derek Bentley
- open prisons.

You **must** also use information of your own.

Part 5: Whitechapel, c1870–c1900: crime, policing and the inner city

5.1 How do we know about crime and policing in Whitechapel, c1870–c1900?

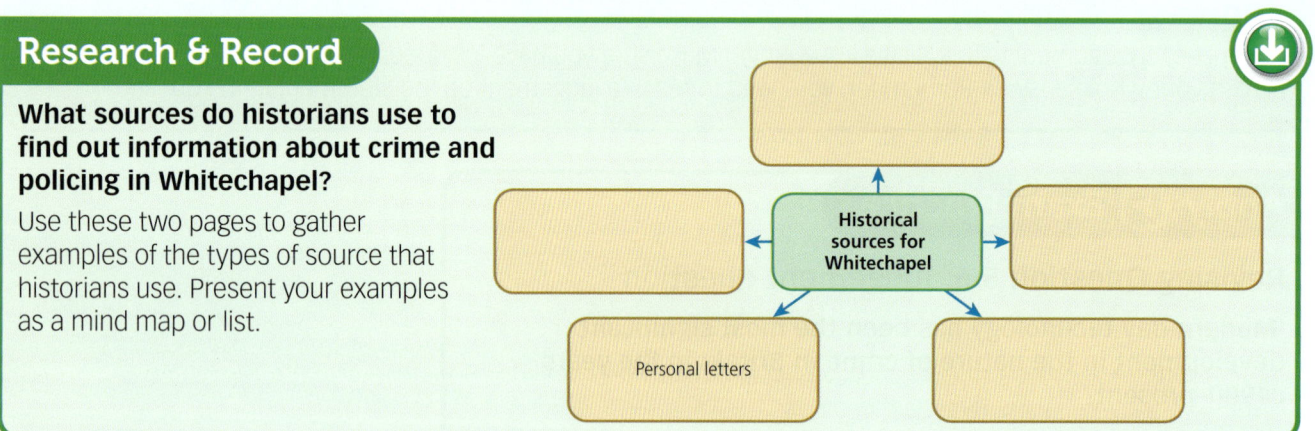

Research & Record

What sources do historians use to find out information about crime and policing in Whitechapel?

Use these two pages to gather examples of the types of source that historians use. Present your examples as a mind map or list.

In this part of your course, you are going to study the Whitechapel area of London in the latter part of the nineteenth century (1800s). The area was densely populated and mostly poor, and you will be investigating the social conditions, the crime which resulted from these conditions and how crimes were tackled. You will be explaining how sources are useful for your study. You will also think about how you might further investigate particular aspects of the topics.

'Sources' is the term we use for anything that historians can gain information from. Historians use a great many written (and drawn) sources. These could be official documents, but could also be personal letters, diaries, newspaper articles, cartoons drawings, song lyrics, tax bills – almost anything. Historians sometimes use artefacts as well. These are objects which shed light on some aspects of the past.

What makes sources useful?

In your exam paper you will get a question about sources. You will be asked to study some and explain how useful they are.

Historians do this too. However, there is an important point to realise here. Historians do not ask whether a source is useful, they ask *how* it is useful. In other words, all sources are useful as evidence about something. Historians make a source useful by using the content and provenance of the source alongside their own knowledge.

Content

Historians make observations and inferences from the content of a source. Observations are what we can read or see in the source – what it says. Inferences are what we find out from the source that it may not tell us directly – what we can infer.

Provenance

Historians consider the provenance of a source, that is the type of source (nature), who created the source and when (origin), and why the source was created (purpose).

Knowledge

Historians compare the content of the source with their own knowledge and use their own knowledge to understand the importance of the provenance. For example, if a source was created in the autumn of 1888 in Whitechapel, a historian would know that this was during the time of the Jack the Ripper murders (see pages 126–29).

What types of sources can be used?

In 2019, the historian Hallie Rubenhold published a bestselling history book about the five known women victims of the murderer Jack the Ripper titled *The Five*. Rubenhold wanted to make her book about the lives of the women, not their deaths. She wanted to reconstruct as much of their lives as she could – the good and the bad. She also wanted to be clear and open about which sources she used and how she used them. Here are just a few:

- Personal letters, for example from family members, public officials
- Official letters by government employees or police officers
- Memoirs, diaries and personal stories
- Social investigations into living conditions and crime, such as Charles Booth's survey
- Old Bailey records of trials
- *Punch* cartoons
- Paintings and photographs
- Medical records, including autopsies
- Reports of coroners' inquests
- Records of crimes and police investigations
- National and local newspapers and magazines
- Employment records and contracts showing wages, deductions, etc.
- Census returns showing who lived in particular houses
- Council records

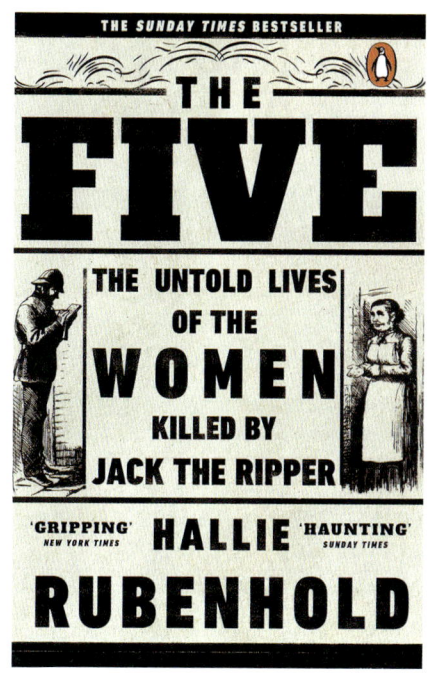

▲ **Source A** *The Five: the untold lives of the women killed by Jack the Ripper* by Hallie Rubenhold

Rubenhold also lists the various archives and record collections she found useful:

- The National Archives is where all documents produced by the British government are kept. This includes all the records of the Metropolitan Police and the Home Office.
- The London Archives holds all records of births, deaths, burials and census returns for Greater London.
- The British Newspaper Archive contains magazines, journals, posters, works of art and many other sources, as well as newspapers.
- The London School of Economics holds (online) the work of the pioneering social researcher Charles Booth, who produced maps showing crime and poverty in London in the 1880s.

Historians like Rubenhold try to use as many different types of sources as possible. This is because sources provide information about the past that helps us understand what life was like at the time. When we use a range of sources, we can begin to build a picture of what life was like for the residents of Whitechapel in the late nineteenth century. However, if we narrow down our enquiry to focus on one aspect of Whitechapel, we need to know and understand which sources are relevant to our chosen enquiry focus. For example, Old Bailey records are very useful for an enquiry into the types of crime committed, but they do not help us fully understand the living conditions or levels of poverty experienced in Whitechapel at the time.

5.2 The local context: Whitechapel c1870–c1900

Research & Record

How did environmental and social problems affect crime in Whitechapel c1870–c1900?

Next you are going to look at the environment and social problems that affected Whitechapel. It is important to understand how these problems affected crime. Use a table like this to record details of the factors.

Factor	Key features	Link between this factor and crime
Overcrowding		
Housing		
Provision for the poor		

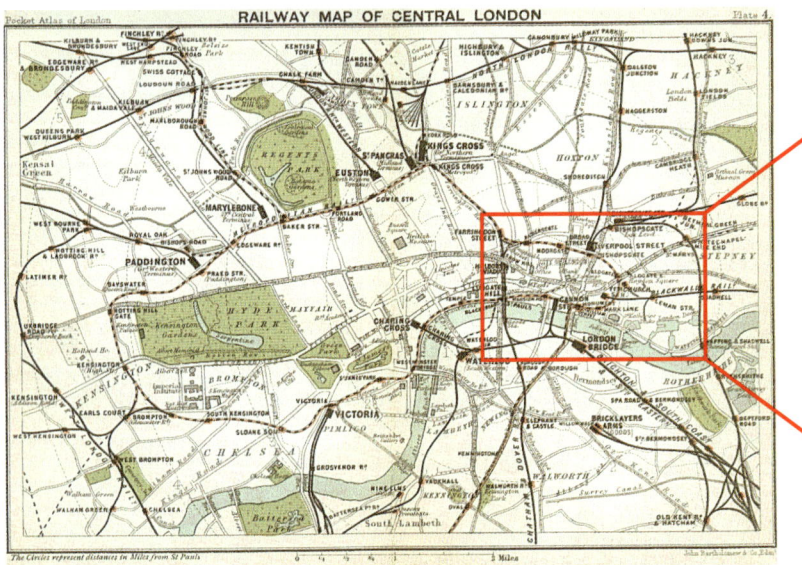

▲ The East End

▲ **Source B** Map of central London in 1899. On the left (in the west) there are areas of open, green parkland; on the right (the East End) is a built-up, industrial space with few green spaces

Whitechapel is an area in the east of London. In the late nineteenth century, it was one of the city's poorest districts. It was overcrowded, dirty and dangerous. Maps like this are useful for understanding some of the context of Whitechapel in the late nineteenth century. We can see:

- many signs of heavy industry – with the large London docks and many rail links to transport materials and goods
- lots of small streets and many buildings with few green or open spaces. This indicates densely packed housing.

London, like other cities and towns in Britain during the nineteenth century, was impacted by industrialisation and population growth. These particularly affected the East End, including Whitechapel.

Impact of industrialisation

New factories and workshops had been springing up in towns and cities since the mid-1700s and in some areas new towns and cities had grown around newly built factories and industries. People flocked to industrialised areas in search of employment. In the East End of London, the industries of shipbuilding, engineering, brewing and printing were booming. They employed thousands of workers, many of whom lived close to their workplaces. Whitechapel was very close to the East London Docks, which was a major source of employment for residents, although jobs were often inconsistent as numbers of exported and imported goods could vary.

The period of industrialisation did not mean that everyone found employment. Often, more people moved into towns and cities than the local economy could support and this meant there was an increase in unemployment and poverty. Whitechapel had high rates of underemployment due to variable employment rates from seasonal work or economic fluctuations. This meant that people were able to find work on some days, such as when the docks were particularly busy with import and exports, but were not needed on other days, leading to economic instability. Those who were employed were poorly paid.

Britain rapidly changed from being a society in which most people lived in the countryside and worked on the land to an industrial society where most people worked in factories and lived in cities. This urban growth was not managed. The result was that many areas of Britain's cities were massively overcrowded. As thousands of people crammed into areas built for much smaller numbers, housing and infrastructure could not cope and **slum areas** developed. As a result, disease and poor health flourished. Crime such as theft became easier to commit and it was harder to catch criminals.

Census records

Census records are one of the most important sources for historians. They help show the impact of industrialisation because they give information on where people lived, how many people lived at an address, who those members of the household were, and their ages and occupations. A census is recorded in England and Wales every ten years, which means historians can compare data and learn how an area has changed over time.

▲ **Source C** An entry from the Whitechapel census of 1881

The problems of housing and overcrowding

As we have seen, industrialisation brought poor living conditions in the poor areas of towns and cities. Slum areas, known as rookeries developed.

Rookeries

There were many rookeries in Whitechapel which housed some of the poorest residents. They comprised buildings of a few storeys which were divided into several apartments. Up to 30 people rented one apartment with many people sharing rooms, beds and toilets. In 1877, one building in a Whitechapel rookery contained 123 rooms, with accommodation for 757 people. Rookeries were separated by courts (small open communal spaces) and alleys which created pathways between them. Both were poorly lit and created opportunity for crimes such as pickpocketing.

In addition to being overcrowded, rookeries were poorly ventilated. There were no sewers, so waste ran directly into the streets and rubbish collections and street cleaning happened very rarely. Many of the families that lived in Whitechapel's rookeries hovered just above or on the poverty line. Those on the lowest incomes generally could only afford the poorest accommodation. Some could not afford to rent permanent housing at all.

> ▼ **Source D** From *The Bitter Cry of Outcast London* by Andrew Mearns, published in 1883. Mearns was a late nineteenth-century social reformer. His pamphlet was an exposé on living conditions in London and ended with a call for reform.
>
> That people condemned to exist under such conditions take to drink and fall into sin is surely a matter of little surprise … One of the saddest results of this overcrowding is the inevitable association of honest people with criminals. Often is the family of an honest working man compelled to take refuge in a thieves' kitchen … Who can wonder that every evil flourishes in such hotbeds of vice and disease?

Apply ▶ Exam Practice

Question 1 style

Describe **one** feature of life in Whitechapel rookeries. (2 marks)

Exam Tip

Question 1a and 1b: Describe one feature …

1. Some students struggle with how to start their answer. Start your answer by **using the key phrase in the question**. This should help you to focus on the question as well as to get started.
2. Do not simply identify a feature of life in Whitechapel rookeries. You need to **develop the feature** that you identify with some **description**.

◀ **Source E** Wentworth Street c1870, by Gustave Doré

Apply ▶ Exam Practice

Question 2a style

How useful are Sources D and E for an enquiry into the problems caused by overcrowded housing in Whitechapel? (8 marks)

Exam Tip

Question 2a: How useful are Sources D and E …?

Your exam will have a source-based question.

- You need to analyse both sources carefully, identifying what they tell you so you can explain why they are useful.
- You have just over 10 minutes to answer this question in the exam. One paragraph for each source is enough for a high-level answer.
- You should focus on how the sources are useful for the enquiry in the question. For example, *Source A is useful because it* … The examiner does not want you to highlight problems with the sources.

In the rest of your paragraph, develop and support your argument by referring to the **content** and **provenance** and your wider **knowledge** of the enquiry. Rememberb this using the CPK method.

C The content of the source

Before you begin to write, highlight/annotate the key information in the source, as we have in Source D on page 108.

P The provenance of the source

Source D was written by Andrew Mearns. Remember, Mearns was a nineteenth-century social reformer. He wrote the pamphlet as an exposé of living conditions in London with the intention of provoking a reaction to call for social reform. The source, therefore, may exaggerate the problems so that Mearns can gain more support for social reform.

Source E was drawn by Gustave Doré. Look at page 110 for information about this artist.

K Your own knowledge of the period

You will need to bring in your own knowledge to explain how the source is useful for the enquiry in the question. Remember that:

- overcrowded slum areas housed some of Whitechapel's poorest residents
- many of the people living in rookeries hovered just above or on the poverty line.

Social reformers

Some people at the time were very concerned about how people lived in slum areas such as Whitechapel. They wrote books and newspaper articles (see Source D), took photographs and drew pictures (see Source E) and carried out surveys to record the living conditions in order to campaign for change.

Booth's survey

Charles Booth is a well-known English social researcher and reformer. He documented working-class life in London and, in 1889, the results of his research were published entitled 'Life and Labour of the People in London'. His report included a map which used colour coding to show different levels of wealth and criminality. Booth and his team conducted the research for the report by visiting households, asking residents to complete surveys and interviewing people. From these he gathered information about poverty levels, however his report on criminality was not based on criminal statistics, but rather a set of assumptions that linked poorer areas to crime.

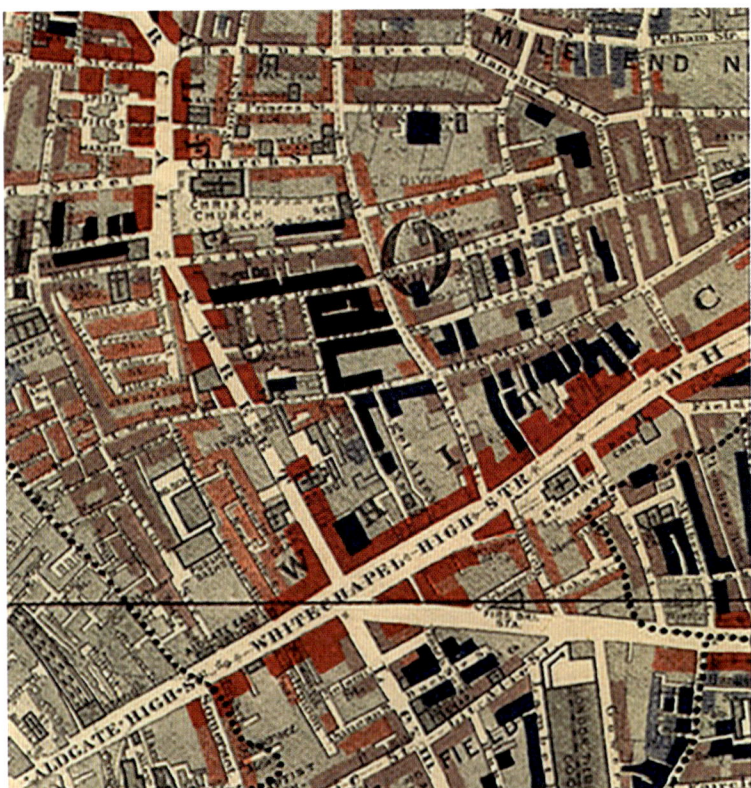

▲ **Source F** Charles Booth's poverty map used colour coding to show different levels of wealth and criminality. Dark colours indicate the poorest areas and suggested that they were most likely to be associated with crime. This section shows Whitechapel

Booth's poverty map is still useful today for historians investigating the link between poverty and crime. However, it cannot explain why some areas experienced such high levels of poverty or overcrowding and historians need additional sources and knowledge to determine how accurate it is, particularly in relation to crime.

Gustave Doré

In 1872, French artist Gustave Doré published a set of illustrations entitled 'London: A Pilgrimage'. Over a period of four years, Doré had toured London alongside British journalist Blanchard Jerrold, often with a police escort in the most dangerous areas, to document the deprivation and squalor of Victorian London. His images (see Source E on page 109) provide a powerful visual record of London that historians can cross-reference alongside other sources to build a picture of how people lived in London in the late nineteenth century.

Revision Tip

Question 2b in your exam asks you to plan a follow-up enquiry from one of the two sources provided. It is important that you can select the right kind of source to develop the specific enquiry given. For example, Gustave Doré's illustrations are excellent sources to follow up the enquiry of living conditions in Whitechapel slums. But they would not help a historian to develop an enquiry focused on conditions within the workhouse.

You can prepare for your exam by understanding the strengths and weaknesses of different types of sources for different enquiries.

Lodging houses

People who experienced the most extreme levels of poverty could only afford cheap accommodation on a night-by-night basis or were homeless, and they struggled to feed themselves and their families. Lodging houses (sometimes referred to as 'doss houses') offered temporary accommodation that could be paid for daily. They offered a bed in a dormitory with other people and the use of a communal kitchen. To accommodate the maximum number of people, some lodging houses operated a shift pattern, offering three eight-hour slots so that beds could be used by up to three different people a day, with no cleaning in between. Landlords often had more than one lodging house, so a deputy would be employed to oversee the collection of rent and management of the house.

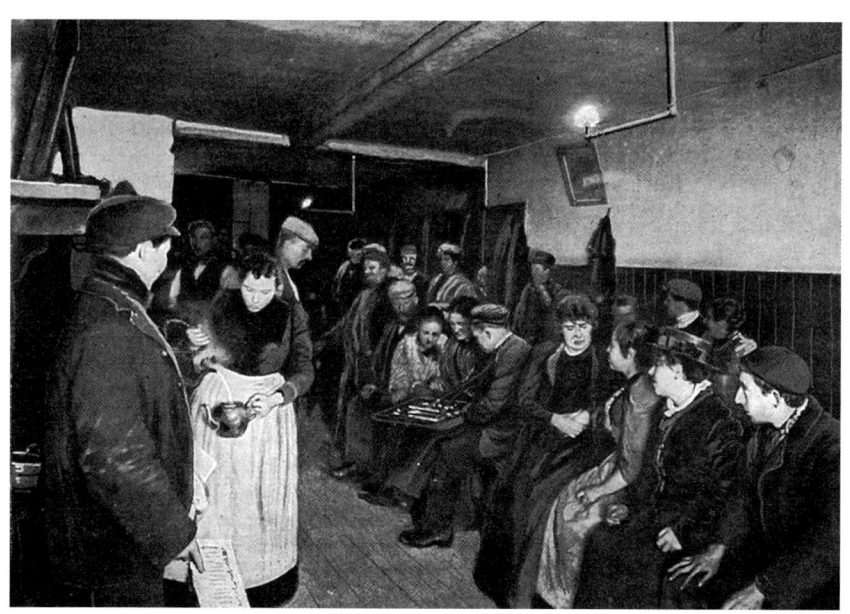

▲ **Source G** Life in an East End lodging house

Conditions were often poor. They were frequently inhabited by rats as well as lodgers and they developed a reputation for being dens of crime and immorality, with men, women and children often mixed in one room.

The Peabody Estate

The government did make some effort to improve housing in areas with high levels of poverty. In 1875 the Artisans' and Labourers' Dwellings Improvement Act was passed. This gave power to the Metropolitan Board of Works (local government for London) to find organisations that would replace slum areas with model housing – purpose-built apartments or estates which provided decent living accommodation for the working class. One of the organisations chosen for the slum clearance programme was the Peabody Trust. The trust was named after (and funded by) the wealthy American merchant and philanthropist George Peabody, who lived in London at the time.

The chosen site for the Peabody Estate had previously been a maze of narrow courtyards, which was cleared and replaced with healthy and suitable housing. The estate was made up of 11 blocks, providing 286 flats and opening in 1881. The flats were intended to be affordable housing and offered modern facilities for tenants.

Provision for the poor in the Whitechapel workhouses

As a last resort, the residents of Whitechapel could turn to the workhouse. In 1834, the Poor Law Amendment Act reformed existing workhouse provision by creating a system of workhouses across Britain to provide poor relief for those who were too poor or sick to survive in the community.

Conditions were deliberately tough. Families were split up on arrival and sent to different wards for men, women and children. They could be punished for trying to talk to each other. Inmates were given a uniform and expected to undertake tough manual labour in return for their bed and board. The system was designed to encourage people to survive through their own means by putting them off entering the workhouse. But regular, well-paid employment was difficult to find and the cycle of poverty was tough to break, so many people found themselves in and out of workhouses as a necessity just to survive.

> ▼ **Source H** An extract from *The People of the Abyss* by Jack London, an American novelist who stayed in doss houses and workhouses in London to see what they were like. In 1902, he visited the Whitechapel casual ward.
>
> Some were set to scrubbing and cleaning, others to picking oakum, and eight of us were convoyed across the street to the Whitechapel Infirmary, where we were set at scavenger work[1]. This was the method by which we paid for our skilly[2] and canvas[3], and I, for one, know that I paid in full many times over.
>
> Though we had most revolting tasks to perform, our allotment was considered the best, and the other men deemed themselves lucky in being chosen to perform it.
>
> 'Don't touch it, mate, the nurse sez it's deadly,' warned my working partner, as I held open a sack into which he was emptying a garbage can.
>
> It came from the sick wards, and I told him that I purposed neither to touch it, nor to allow it to touch me. Nevertheless, I had to carry the sack, and other sacks, down five flights of stairs and empty them in a receptacle where the corruption was speedily sprinkled with strong disinfectant.
>
> [1] **scavenger work** – street cleaning.
> [2] **skilly** – a kind of weak broth or soup made from water, vegetables and cornflour.
> [3] **canvas** – this means the use of a hammock as a bed for the night.

▲ **Source I** A painting of people lining up to be admitted to an East End casual ward. Published in the *Penny Illustrated Paper*, 15 September 1888

Unlike the grim, filthy conditions of the rookeries, workhouses were notoriously clean. Inmates were made to strip and bath upon arrival and many of the chores they performed involved scrubbing and cleaning to keep disease from spreading among inmates.

Some workhouses offered casual wards where vagrants could spend short periods while they tried to find other help. The largest workhouse in Whitechapel was in St Thomas Street and it had a grim reputation. It was a casual ward, so only allowed short stays. Those who were desperate could enter at 4 p.m. and were discharged at 6 a.m. They had to obey strict rules and work at tasks such as oakum picking (breaking down old rope into fibres) or breaking rocks.

Workhouses kept records of those who were admitted into casual wards or for longer stays. This enables historians to see the names of those who used them, the frequency with which they visited and the kind of work they completed while they were there. Conditions were also publicised in newspapers and magazines, such as the *Penny Illustrated Paper* which was published weekly and featured sketches like Source I.

Connect and Engage

1. How is Source I, an image from the *Penny Illustrated Paper*, useful to a historian wanting to learn more about the casual ward at the workhouse?
2. What do we need to be aware of when using sources from newspapers and magazines?

▲ **Source J** A group of men picking oakum in return for a night's stay at St Thomas Street Casual Ward

Apply ▶ Exam Practice

1a/b Describe **one** feature of life in the workhouse. (2 marks)

2a How useful are Sources H and J for an enquiry into the nature of casual wards in Whitechapel workhouses during the late nineteenth century?

Explain your answer using Sources H and J and your knowledge of the historical context. (8 marks)

Exam Tip

Question 2a: CKP

Remind yourself of the CPK advice on page 109 about how to approach this type of question.

C Look carefully at the **content** of the sources. Explain what we can learn from the sources about the experiences of inmates in Whitechapel workhouses.

K Use your contextual **knowledge**. Source H describes the experiences of Jack London, who visited the Whitechapel casual ward in 1902 to understand what life was like for inmates there. Source J shows men picking oakum in return for a night's stay at St Thomas Street casual ward. Can you remember the location and purpose of St Thomas Street casual ward? If you can't, look back at page 113 before you plan your answer.

P Use the **provenance** of the sources. Explain why the nature/author of each of the sources is useful for this enquiry and link to the content. Source H is written by Jack London and it will be useful for this enquiry because the author describes his experiences and interactions with other inmates during his visit to the casual ward in Whitechapel. His descriptions of the work he carried out and things he witnessed are useful for understanding the nature of casual wards at the time.

Exam Tip

Use connectives and evidence for stronger arguments

When explaining how a source is useful for an enquiry, you need to prove that the source is useful. For example:

Sample answer

Source H is useful for an enquiry into the nature of casual wards in Whitechapel workhouses because it tells us about the nature of the living conditions and work that inhabitants could expect. The source is useful because it tells us that there were several different tasks that people inside the casual ward were expected to do. Jack London states that 'Some were set to scrubbing and cleaning, others to picking oakum, and eight of us were convoyed across the street to the Whitechapel Infirmary, where we were set at scavenger work'. He goes on to explain that this work was essential as 'this was the method by which we paid for our skilly and canvas'. This tells us that people within the casual ward were expected to complete hard and often physical work to earn their food and bed for the night. The nature of Source H is useful for an enquiry into the nature of casual wards in Whitechapel workhouses because it is a first-hand account written by a man who stayed in doss houses and workhouses to investigate the conditions. His account gives an important overview of the conditions within casual wards, which is accurate because casual wards only admitted people for one night, and the strict rules meant that they were expected to earn their keep by undertaking work such as oakum picking.

Source J is useful ...

Use connectives to link your arguments to the enquiry

Phrases like 'is useful for an enquiry into', 'this tells us' and 'this shows' are called connectives because they link your arguments to the enquiry and so help you prove how the source is useful.

Add specific knowledge

Provide evidence to substantiate (support) your argument. Use phrases such as 'for example', 'such as' and 'this demonstrates' to introduce or flag your supporting evidence.

5.3 The inhabitants of Whitechapel

Research & Record

What factors impacted on who lived in Whitechapel and how did these affect the local environment?

Use pages 116–119 to complete your own copy of this table about the inhabitants of Whitechapel in the late nineteenth century.

Feature	Who this attracted to Whitechapel and the effects on the local environment
Low-paid and insecure work	Poorest workers – working and living in squalid conditions
Fluctuating population	

Lack of secure employment and low wages

People lived in these cramped and unhealthy conditions because they had no real choice. Many of the poorest workers were effectively trapped in Whitechapel where accommodation was cheap and there was at least a chance of work, both of which were harder to find elsewhere. Many worked in sweatshops undertaking tasks such as tailoring, shoe making and making matches. Working conditions were cramped, poorly ventilated and had very little natural light. Others worked as labourers in the nearby London docks, or in railway construction, very physical work which was not always guaranteed day by day. Workers had to be close at hand and constantly on call for when the employers had work for them to do. Lack of jobs and job security as well as low wages meant many lived in poverty.

> ▼ **Source K** An extract from the report of the Royal Commission on the Housing of the Working Classes, 1884–85
>
> Workers are trapped near their places of employment. For example, there are the women who must take their work home, such as those who work for the City tailors; and the girls who are employed in small factories, such as those for artificial flowers; these also have to be in attendance morning after morning (like their husbands and brothers working on the docks) whether there is work for them or not, for if they are not within calling distance, they lose it.

A fluctuating population

As we have seen, many could not afford permanent accommodation or frequently moved from place to place looking for work or to be closer to their temporary job. Many relied on lodging houses or pubs, which also let rooms. Flower and Dean Street was a well-known rookery where numerous doss houses in squalid conditions could be found. The 1871 census showed that there were 902 lodgers staying in 31 lodging houses on this street alone.

There was also increased immigration into big cities at this time. Charles Booth's survey concluded that between 1871 and 1891 around 850,000 people had moved to London from other parts of Britain and approximately 75,000 had migrated to London from other countries. Many came from Ireland and Eastern Europe. They arrived with little money and so were forced to live in areas like Whitechapel and often in lodging houses and pubs.

As a result, the population was constantly changing with few people having ties to the local community. This created tensions and hostility which sometimes led to violence.

Irish migration

There was large-scale migration from Ireland into Britain throughout the second half of the 1800s. It began with the disastrous famine of the 1840s in Ireland which killed around 1 million people and forced another 1.5 million to emigrate. From that point on, emigration became a feature of life in Ireland. Many went to North America, but many thousands came to British towns and cities. Irish immigrants made up about 22 per cent of the immigrants living in Whitechapel in the 1870s and 1880s. Most were unskilled labourers. The men competed with other immigrants and local labourers for work on the docks and other casual work. Some men worked as 'navvies' (navigators), building the new railway lines in East London. The women tended to work in sweatshops or laundries or as domestic servants.

Irish immigrants faced a huge amount of prejudice and discrimination. Many local people blamed immigrants for taking away their own job opportunities. Irish people were also competing with other immigrants for jobs and this increased tensions as well. Another factor was that most of the Irish immigrants were Catholics and there was still a great deal of prejudice and suspicion towards them in the late 1800s stemming from ongoing serious tension between Protestants and Catholics.

◀ **Source L** Irish navvies working on the Metropolitan Railway line during the construction of the Midland Railway's extension to St Pancras in the 1860s

▲ **Source M** Debris from a wall blown into the street by an explosion set by the Fenians, which occurred at Scotland Yard, May 1884

Another factor which caused tension was the actions of a militant Irish group called the Fenians (see page 50). At this time, Britain ruled all of Ireland. The Fenians wanted independence from Britain and they were prepared to use violence to make it happen. They carried out a number of violent attacks in Ireland but also in Britain. From 1881 to 1884, they were responsible for around 20 bomb attacks in different cities. The vast majority of Irish immigrants had nothing to do with these attacks, but this did not stop them being treated with resentment and suspicion.

Jewish migration

There had been a Jewish community in London since the 1600s, but in the 1880s the Jewish population expanded rapidly. The main reason was that Jewish people, particularly in the Russian Empire, were facing persecution because of their faith. Many of them fled to England and a very large proportion of them settled in Whitechapel.

Like other immigrants, the majority faced a daily struggle with poverty and hardship. Many of them worked in the clothing trade. As with many **immigrant** groups, they worked incredibly hard, often in poor conditions, and usually received lower wages than other people in the community. Jewish cloth makers often worked in 'sweatshops', in cramped conditions for long hours and low wages.

As with other immigrant groups, Jewish people in Whitechapel faced hostility and prejudice. They were competing with other workers for jobs and so they were resented. They were marked out by their religious beliefs, which differed from those of the majority. Many did not speak English. Jewish migrants often lived in close-knit communities, maintaining strong cultural and social ties, which sometimes resulted in less integration with the wider population. This also helped to protect them from the frequent hostility, prejudice and violence they faced.

The map (Source N) shows areas of Whitechapel where Jewish people lived highlighted in blue. It was published in *The Jew in London: a study of racial character and present-day conditions*. In the introduction, social reformer Samuel Barnett wrote that he hoped the publication would 'do away with the prejudices which are founded either on ... jealousy of the Jews' success or on the ignorance which is irritated at their different habits and opinions.'

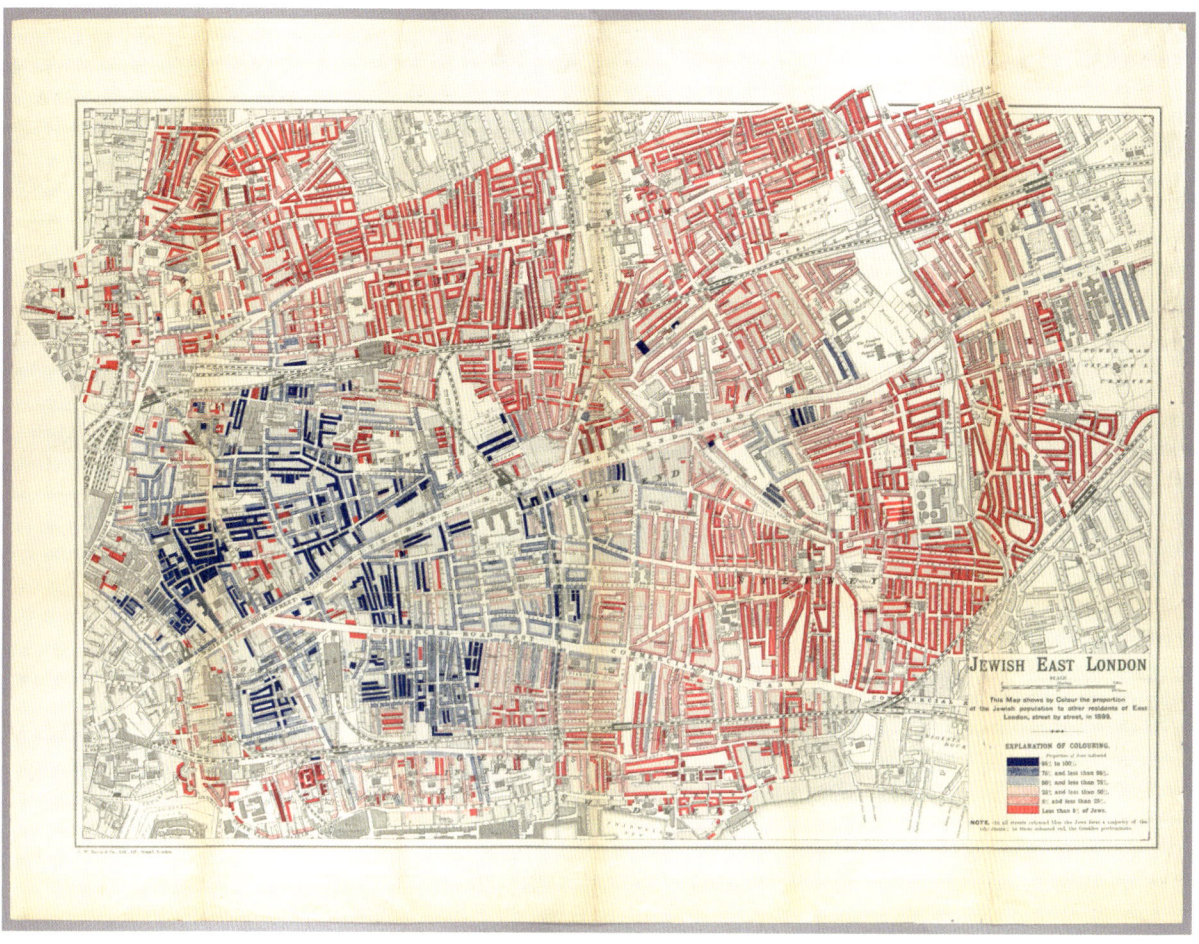

▲ **Source N** George Arkell's 1899 colour-coded map of Spitalfields and Whitechapel in the East End. Blue areas indicate a majority of residents were Jewish

Another factor which led to suspicion was that Jewish immigrants tended to unite and look after each other. For example, in 1885, the Jewish community created the Jews' Temporary Shelter. It was similar to the lodging houses in London but it only looked after Jewish people and it also helped recent immigrants to the area make a start in their new life. There was also a free school set up for Jewish children. An even more high-profile example of Jewish people helping others in their community was, in 1887, when the Rothschild family built apartments similar to the Peabody blocks to help Jewish immigrants find accommodation. Today, it might seem obvious that the Jewish community would do this. But to a hostile population competing for housing and work, it was easy to believe that Jewish people sought to improve their own situation at the expense of others.

Apply ▶ Exam Practice

2a How useful are Sources M and N for an enquiry into tensions as a result of immigration into Whitechapel?

Explain your answer using Sources M and N and your knowledge of the historical context. **(8 marks)**

5.4 The national and regional context

> ### Research & Record
>
> **Who was responsible for investigating crime in Whitechapel?**
>
> Your knowledge from Chapter 3.4 The nature of law enforcement c1700–c1900 will support your understanding of the national context.
>
> Use pages 120–21 to complete your own copy of this table, which will help you find specific information about the nature and problems of policing Whitechapel.
>
> | Key question | Answer |
> |---|---|
> | Who directed the Metropolitan Police Force? | |
> | What were the attitudes of the public towards the police? | |
> | What was the quality of police recruits? | |
> | Why was the CID set up in 1878? | |

Policing London in the late nineteenth century

There were two police forces responsible for London.

- Most of London was policed by the Metropolitan Police Force. Unlike other police forces which were run by local authorities, the Met was directed by the national government. It reported directly to the Home Secretary – who also appointed the head of the force.
- The City of London police was responsible for policing the square mile-sized district of London known as the City of London, an important business and financial district.

The two forces were meant to work together, but communication was often poor and they generally considered themselves to be rivals. The Met was the largest police force in Britain at the time. However, there were still fewer than 14,000 police officers policing a population of over 5 million people.

Commissioner Sir Charles Warren

In 1886, after a period of political unrest and demonstrations, the Home Secretary appointed Sir Charles Warren as Metropolitan Police Commissioner. Warren had enjoyed a highly successful career in the military and he believed in military-style discipline. He recruited more ex-soldiers into the Met police and introduced more military-style drilling into their training.

His first real test came in November 1887 when a march in Trafalgar Square was organised to protest about unemployment and British rule in Ireland. Many from Whitechapel took part in the march and Whitechapel police officers were among the police that day. Warren called in the army to support the police. It became known as Bloody Sunday as the march erupted into a violent battle which left many injured. Some people felt it showed the police did not support the poor and Warren became extremely unpopular in poorer parts of London. Warren was forced out as commissioner in 1888 due to the police's failure to catch the person responsible for the Ripper murders (see pages 126–29).

The development of CID

In 1842, a detective department was added to the Metropolitan Police. It was small and ineffective, mostly because there was confusion over whether detectives should prevent or detect crime. Throughout the 1860s and 1870s, there was a focus on trying to improve the quality of the Metropolitan Police Force. Policing was a difficult and dangerous job. Many people still resented or disliked the police. There were also not enough police constables to tackle the amount of crime happening in London. This, in turn, made it difficult to get good recruits.

There were also problems within the force with alcohol and avoiding work. For example, in 1863, 215 officers were dismissed for being drunk on duty. There were also some high-profile scandals involving dishonesty or corruption. The most serious was in 1877, when several senior detectives were found guilty of corruption, helping criminals with fraud and illegal gambling. In response to this, the Commissioner (Edmund Henderson) appointed a lawyer, Howard Vincent, to reform the detective service. Vincent set up the Criminal Investigation Department (CID) in 1878.

▲ **Source O** The Bloody Sunday riots in 1887

The CID had over 200 officers and a clear purpose – to detect crime. The officers wore plain clothes, used surveillance techniques and followed suspects around. This might sound like effective policing, but to many people it felt more like an oppressive government trying to limit people's freedom. In 1883, a Special Irish Branch was set up to monitor the Irish Republican Brotherhood (also known as Fenians). In 1887, Sir Robert Anderson was appointed as head of CID. He would work alongside Sir Charles Warren during the investigation of the Ripper murders.

Attitudes to the police

There were mixed attitudes to the police. In many areas, most people had come to see the police as reliable and helpful. They wanted good order on the streets and understood that the police helped to protect this. In poorer areas like Whitechapel, the police had a more difficult time earning the respect of the public. They were seen as upholders of the law for an unpopular government, especially after events such as Bloody Sunday.

However, the local authorities viewed the police more as social workers. By the 1870s, a series of government laws had widened the role of the police to include dealing with traffic control, vagrancy, sewage and litter, pubs and accidents. This led to further mixed public reactions to the police.

5.5 The organisation of policing in Whitechapel

Research & Record

How was Whitechapel policed?

Use pages 122–25 to complete this table. For each aspect of policing, record a list of key features and provide a description that expands and explains each feature.

	Key features	Description
H Division		
The role of the beat constable		
Difficulties in policing Whitechapel		
Crime and antisocial behaviour		

Whitechapel was a difficult and often dangerous area to police at this time.

The work of H Division

The Metropolitan Police was organised into 20 separate divisions, each one policing a particular area of London. Whitechapel was the responsibility of H Division. H Division had about 500 ordinary constables. They were supervised by 37 sergeants. Above the sergeants were 27 inspectors and the commanders of the division were a superintendent and a chief inspector.

The main job of the constable was to patrol the streets, but in Whitechapel high levels of poverty led to police conducting aspects of social work as well as tackling crime. They were often on hand to help charities in their work for poorer people. Police officers accompanied Charles Booth during his research into poverty in London. H Division often hosted soup kitchens to provide food for the poor, which were well received within the community, even if they did have the ulterior motive of trying to get information from witnesses. But attempts to control prostitution were resented by the women who depended on it. The police also had many sad and unpleasant duties which increased their unpopularity and were often met with great hostility. These included evicting tenants who could not pay their rent or escorting desperate people to the workhouse.

The role of the 'beat constable'

Constables were assigned a 'beat' – an area to patrol during their shift for the day or night – and were known as **beat constables**. The main point of this police presence was to deter criminals and make them think twice about committing crime. But it was also partly to reassure local people that the police were present and protecting them. Walking the beat involved:

- stopping and questioning people at night to find out what they were doing
- meeting up with the beat sergeant at certain intervals to report what had happened. The conversation was recorded in his diary
- often boring and sometimes dangerous work.

Pay was relatively poor and constables could be fined or dismissed if they missed a crime on their beat without good reason.

The difficulties of policing Whitechapel

Geography

The geography of Whitechapel made policing extremely difficult. Once away from the main roads, there was a maze of narrow alleys, twisting streets and courtyards. Most of the people who interested the police lived in densely packed rookeries. It was almost impossible to locate a criminal in these areas as they would be alerted long before the police arrived. In any case, people tended not to stay in one place for long periods of time so may have changed address.

Many distrusted the police. Some were openly hostile and police constables were often attacked.

Whitechapel was a breeding ground for crimes, many of which were linked to high levels of poverty and unemployment. People would resort to crime rather than go into the workhouse.

◀ **Source P** A cartoon from *Punch* magazine published in 1888 during the time of the Ripper murders. It highlighted the inadequacies and problems of policing at the time. The policeman is shown wearing a blindfold, playing a game of blindman's buff (a variation of tag where the tagger has their eyes covered), suggesting that policing at the time was ineffective because when trying to detect crime and criminals the police were working in the dark

Alcohol

In Whitechapel, alcohol was cheap and easy to obtain from pubs, gin palaces (a bar known for its lavish décor) or street vendors. Many people used alcohol to forget their poverty, poor health, depression and despair. There are many reports of links between alcohol, social problems and crime. In 1879, the government passed the Habitual Drunkards Act, which allowed the police to take alcoholics to a sanatorium to recover. But there were not enough sanitoriums and far too many people who abused alcohol.

In the case of men, alcohol tended to be linked to violent crime, such as brawls in the street. All too often it meant domestic violence, where men under the influence of alcohol abused their wives and children. It also increased poverty, as wages were spent on drink, and some people committed crimes in search of money to buy more alcohol.

Prostitution

There was a strong connection in many cases between alcohol and prostitution. Prostitution was not illegal but it was a sensitive issue and prostitutes were often caught up in related crimes, such as trying to leave lodgings without paying rent. Lack of employment opportunities meant that some women turned to prostitution in desperation. Many used it as a short-term measure. Prostitutes were vulnerable to abuse, assault, infection and illness.

> ▼ **Source Q** An extract from an article in the *Daily News*, November 1888 titled 'An Autumn Evening in Whitechapel'
>
> Turn down a side street out of the main Whitechapel Road. It may be well to tuck out of view any bit of jewellery that may be showing. The street is oppressively dark. Men are lounging at the doors of the shops, smoking evil-smelling pipes. Women are sauntering about in twos and threes, or are seated gossiping on steps leading into passages dark as the underworld. Now round the corner into another still gloomier passage, for there are no shops here to speak of. This is the notorious Wentworth Street. The police used to make a point of going through this only in couples, and possibly may do so still when they go there at all. Just now there are none to be seen.

Gangs and protection rackets

There were many gangs in the Whitechapel area. Some were immigrant gangs, especially Jewish gangs, who protected themselves and their communities from attacks because attacks on Jewish people were common. There were Irish gangs, as well as gangs from Eastern Europe.

However, the main criminal gangs simply wanted money and engaged in robbery and **protection rackets**. Small traders often had to pay money to prevent a gang from smashing up their businesses. Many criminal gangs forced prostitutes to hand over some of their earnings in return for 'protection'. In reality, this meant giving money so the gangs did not beat or even kill them. The police found it difficult to stop gangs and many residents accused them of not caring because the gangs generally attacked the weaker and poorer members of the community.

Violent demonstrations

There were frequent demonstrations in Whitechapel and in other parts of London that people from Whitechapel took part in. These were very difficult to police with such a small number of officers, and often turned violent (see pages 120–21 on Bloody Sunday).

> ### Exam Tip
>
> **Question 2b style**
>
> In your exam, question 2b will ask you to plan a follow-up enquiry for one of the two sources given on the exam paper. For example:
>
> **2b** How could you follow up Source Q to find out more about the difficulties of policing Whitechapel? (4 marks)
>
> Read Source Q on page 124 again. Then look at the steps below that explain how to answer this type of question.
>
> | Steps | Sample answer |
> |---|---|
> | Select a **detail from the source**. This should be a quotation from a written source or something you can see in a visual source. | Detail in Source Q that I would follow up: 'This is the notorious Wentworth Street.' |
> | Write a **question** that is **linked to the detail above** and would enable you to find out more about **the enquiry in the question**. | Question I would ask: Was Wentworth Street more problematic to police than other areas of Whitechapel? |
> | Select a **contemporary source** that will give you the answer to your question. Make it **specific** to Whitechapel. | What type of source I could use: H Division police records |
> | **Explain how** the source you have chosen will answer your question. | How this might help answer my question: These records will contain details of crimes and the arrests made by H Division and would enable me to compare the nature and frequency of crime in Wentworth Street compared to other areas of Whitechapel. |

5.6 Investigative policing in Whitechapel

Research & Record

How did the police investigate the murders of Jack the Ripper and what difficulties did they have?

Use a table like this to record details of how the police investigated the murders of Jack the Ripper and the problems they encountered in doing so.

Factor	Details
Techniques of investigative policing	
The problem of evidence	
Co-operation between forces	
Problems caused by the media reporting	
The Whitechapel Vigilance Committee	

Developments in techniques of investigative policing

By the time of the Ripper murders most detectives at the CID were using Sir Howard Vincent's Police Code, which made many recommendations:

- Detectives carried out interviews with victims, witnesses and suspects and kept detailed notes.
- Detailed searches of crime scenes were carried out, including the clothing and possessions of murder victims and everything was recorded carefully.
- Detectives started using sketches of wanted criminals, usually based on descriptions from victims or witnesses. As the new technology of photography developed, detectives made increasing use of it to add to their records on crime scenes and criminals.
- Police began to make increasing use of expert witnesses, particularly medical experts who could give an opinion on time of death and possible weapon(s) used.

The Jack the Ripper murders

In the autumn of 1888, a series of murders was carried out in Whitechapel that were extremely shocking and brutal. The murderer became known as Jack the Ripper.

Whitechapel's H Division received a huge amount of criticism for its failure to arrest the Ripper. Many historians now think that this criticism is excessively harsh. The reality was that H Division simply did not have the resources to tackle the investigation. The Metropolitan Police transferred around 50 constables from other divisions of the Met to H Division to provide more manpower. The police carried out over 2000 interviews, distributed 80,000 notices around the city asking for witnesses or information and investigated around 300 suspects.

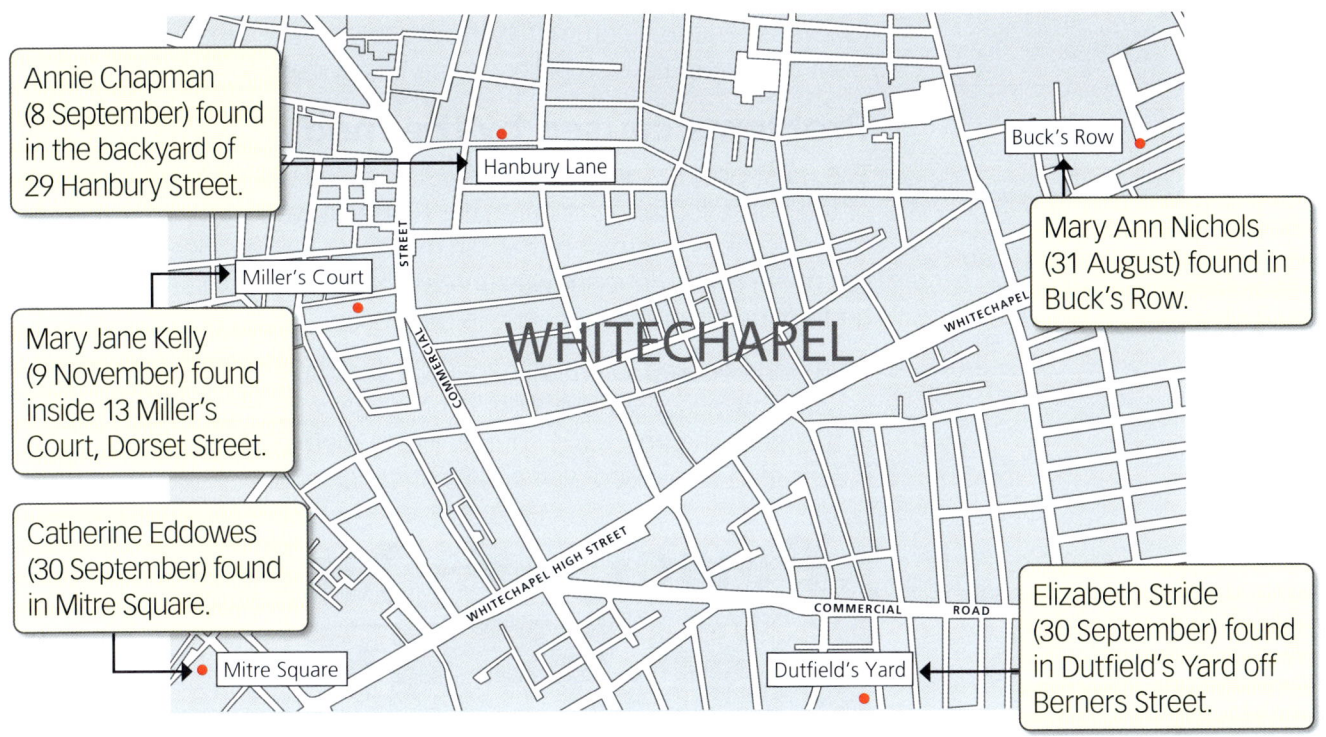

▲ Map showing where the Ripper's victims were found

The problem of evidence

The victims were killed in dark, isolated places, mostly in the dead of night. Not surprisingly, there were no reliable witnesses. The police were overwhelmed by a huge number of letters and witness statements. Many of them were well meaning but wrong. There was one set of letters which were sent to the police and published, and it was these that actually first used the name 'Jack the Ripper'. The police published these letters in the hope of gaining some leads, but they did not help the investigation.

One theory was that the Ripper might have medical experience because of the ways some of the bodies were cut up. Once again, there was no strong evidence to support this theory, and it resulted in a great deal of speculation and wasted time.

Problems caused by the need for cooperation between police forces

Catherine Eddowes was discovered in an area looked after by the City of London police. The others were all under the jurisdiction of the Met. While many officers from the Met and the City of London police generally worked well together, there were high-profile disagreements between Scotland Yard (Metropolitan Police headquarters) and leaders of the City of London police, which did not help public confidence in the investigation. For example, Warren was opposed to offering a reward for information about the murders. However, the City of London police did offer a reward of £500 (over £80,000 today).

Each force undoubtedly wanted to be the one that arrested the Ripper and there were rumours that evidence was withheld from each other. For example, Warren ordered antisemitic graffiti discovered near the scene of Catherine Eddowes' murder to be removed before it could be photographed. He was worried that it would cause violence towards the Jewish community. However, some felt that he did not want the City of London police to see this evidence.

Problems caused by the media

The most obvious problem the media caused was in its criticism of the police for failing to catch the Ripper. It was understandable that there was frustration that the murderer had not been caught, but much of the criticism was unreasonable and unfair, and it undermined public confidence in the police.

Journalists flocked to Whitechapel. They wrote up all the most sensational accounts they could find, usually from talking to people in the area. The police did not talk to the media so any gaps in the information were filled with gossip or speculation.

▶ **Source R** The front page of *The Illustrated Police News*, October 1888. The title suggests it was a police publication, but in fact it was a commercial newspaper which focused on crime stories. The caption reads: 'Two more Whitechapel horrors. When will the murderer be captured?'

The results were predictable and unpleasant. The reporting created a sense of panic and unease. This suited the newspapers because panic meant people wanted more information and so bought more newspapers. And so a vicious circle developed into a mass panic and was soon followed by attacks on innocent individuals suddenly accused of being the Ripper. These attacks were often fuelled by pre-existing prejudices against particular groups, especially Jewish people.

The Whitechapel Vigilance Committee

One of the responses to the critical press coverage was the Whitechapel Vigilance Committee. This was formed by a Whitechapel builder called George Lusk. He was so disappointed in the police that he gathered local people onto his committee. They hired two private detectives to look into the Ripper murders. The committee offered a reward for information, directly contradicting the Home Secretary's views. The committee also sent out gangs with flaming torches onto the Whitechapel streets at night, making a great deal of noise to intimidate the Ripper. Despite this, the attacks did not stop and the work of the committee may have even hindered the investigation. They sent thousands of potential leads named by the public to the police, who were duty bound to investigate them all, though many were ludicrous.

> ▼ **Source S** A journalist's eyewitness account of a Vigilance Committee patrol at work on Saturday 15 September 1888
>
> They seem determined to take all the work out of the hands of the police.
>
> The number of Vigilance Committees that have been formed is remarkable.
>
> The duties mapped out for them will be no sinecure[1]. They will consist in patrolling the streets, noting the various beats, watching how the constables work them, seeing that the police pay due attention to suspicious characters, calls for help etc., and, in case of neglect, reporting to headquarters, so that formal communication may be made to the police authorities on the subject.
>
> This applies to the private constables, but a similar watch in a somewhat modified degree will also be kept over the superior officers, who will be liable to be reported at the direction of the Vigilance Committee.
>
> [1] **will be no sincure** – will require hard work and will not be paid.

Apply ▶ Exam Practice

1a/b Describe **one** feature of the Whitechapel Vigilance Committee. (2 marks)

2a How useful are Sources R and S for an enquiry into the problems the police faced when investigating the Ripper murders?
Explain your answer using Sources R and S and your knowledge of the historical context. (8 marks)

2b How could you follow up Source S to find out more about the problems the police faced when investigating the Ripper murders?

Detail in Source S that I would follow up:
_____

Question I would ask:
_____

What type of source I could use:
_____

How this might help answer my question:
_____

5.7 Whitechapel c1870–c1900 review

Review

How did the nature of Whitechapel impact upon its inhabitants, crime and policing of the area, c1870–c1900?

Copy and complete a table like the one below to review the period. The table has been started to give you some ideas. Do not simply fill in the blanks; also try to add more notes to the other cells.

Theme	Impact on inhabitants	Impact on crime	Impact on policing
The problems of housing and overcrowding	Rookeries Lodging/doss houses Poor sanitation The Peabody Estate High levels of immigrants looking for work / cheap accommodation	High crime rates Anti-social behaviours such as drunkenness	
The lack of employment opportunities and poverty	Seasonal or irregular work Workhouses Charities	Survival crimes such as theft to avoid the workhouse	Setting up of soup kitchens
The impact of migration into the area (immigration) and a fluctuating population without ties to the community	Increased competition for employment		
The work of H Division and the difficulties of policing the slum area of Whitechapel		Protection rackets Gangs Violent demonstrations Attacks on Jewish people	Dark and narrow streets, alleys and courts made policing more difficult
Dealing with the crimes of Jack the Ripper	Formation of the Whitechapel Vigilance Committee		Problems caused by the media reporting the 'Ripper' murders The Whitechapel Vigilance Committee

Revision Tip

When you revise for the historic environment section of your exam, make sure you can describe the features of different types of crime, methods of policing in the area, and the conditions in which people lived and worked.

Apply ▶ Recall Challenges

1 Know the key developments

a How did the Peabody Estate improve living conditions for some Whitechapel residents?
b What did charities do to try and support the poorest residents in Whitechapel?
c Outside of policing duties, what other roles did H Division take on to support residents in the local community?
d What impact did the use of medical experts have on investigations into crimes such as murder?
e How else did investigative policing develop during the period? Which of these developments do you think was the most significant and why?

2 Know the historical sources

Make an A4 copy of this bingo card. You will need plenty of space to write in each box.

Historical sources bingo		
A copy of the *Penny Illustrated Paper*	A diary belonging to a beat constable from H Division	Drawings of the local area, such as those produced by Gustave Doré
Central records from H Division	Records of trials from the Old Bailey	A national newspaper from 1888

a For each historical source, from memory, describe the information that is likely to be included. Then check your answers with your teacher.
b For each historical source, explain how it could be useful for an enquiry into the types of crime committed in Whitechapel.

3 Preparing to answer question 2b

Question 2b in your exam asks you to plan a follow-up enquiry for one of the two sources provided. It is important that you can select the correct kind of source to develop the specific enquiry given.

Prepare for your exam by identifying a range of sources that would be useful for pursuing enquiries about:

- Housing
- Workhouses
- Lodging houses
- Migration/immigration
- Crime
- Policing

5.8 Whitechapel c1870–c1900 exam practice

Apply ▶ Exam Practice

Question 1 style

1a Describe **one** feature of investigative policing used in Whitechapel during the Ripper murders. (2 marks)

1b Describe **one** feature of the problems caused by the media during the investigations into the Ripper murders. (2 marks)

Apply ▶ Exam Practice

Question 2a style

	Key	
Black	Poorest area, people often criminal and violent
Dark blue	Very poor people, often unemployed
Light blue	People poor but they are employed
Pink	People fairly comfortable. Good ordinary earnings
Red	Middle-class people

▲ **Source T** The area of Whitechapel as shown in Charles Booth's survey of London, published in 1889

▼ **Source U** An extract from *The Bitter Cry of Outcast London*, by Reverend Andrew Mearns, published in 1883

Every room in these rotten and reeking tenements houses a family, often two. Some cannot even afford these wretched rooms. They wander about all day, picking up a living as they can, and then take refuge at night in one of the common lodging houses. These are often the resorts of thieves and vagabonds of the lowest type.

2a How useful are sources T and U for an enquiry into levels of poverty in Whitechapel?
Explain your answer using sources T and U and your knowledge of the historical context. (8 marks)

Exam Tip

The usefulness of sources (Question 2a)

Look again at the advice on how to approach this type of question on page 114.
Remember to focus on why the source is useful and to use your knowledge of the focus of the enquiry.

- Consider what the content of each source tells us about levels of poverty in Whitechapel.
- How can you develop this using your own contextual knowledge?
- Consider how the nature (type of source) makes the provenance of the source useful for this enquiry.

Exam Tip

Follow-up enquiry from a source (Question 2b)

Your exam will include a question that asks you to plan a follow-up enquiry from one of the two sources provided.

Look at the steps below that explain how to answer the following question:

2b How could you follow up on Source K (on page 116) to find out more about the link between lack of employment opportunities and poverty? (4 marks)

Steps	Sample answer
Select a **detail from the source**. This should be a quotation from a written source or something you can see in a visual source.	Detail in Source K (page 116) that I would follow up: 'whether there is work for them or not, for if they are not within calling distance, they lose it'.
Write a **question** that is **linked to the detail above** and would enable you to find out more about the enquiry in the question.	Question I would ask: Was it common for those living in poverty in Whitechapel to rely on irregular or seasonal work?
Select a **contemporary source** that will give you the answer to your question. Make it **specific** to Whitechapel c1870–c1900.	What type of source could I use: Census return from the Whitechapel area
Explain how the source you have chosen will answer your question.	How this might help answer my question: These records contain details of the addresses and occupations of people at the time the data was collected. This would enable me to see how many people in Whitechapel relied on irregular work and what type of accommodation they lived in at the time.

Apply ▶ Exam Practice

Question 2 style

2b How could you follow up Source U (on page 132) to find out more about levels of poverty in Whitechapel?

In your answer, you must give the question you would ask and the type of source you could use. (4 marks)

Detail in Source U that I would follow up:
_____

Question I would ask:
_____

What type of source I could use:
_____

How this might help answer my question:
_____

Exam Tip

Follow-up enquiry from a source (Question 2b)

Look again at the advice on how to approach this type of question on page 125.

Remember to focus all parts of your answer on the enquiry in the question.

- Select a quotation from Source H (page 112).
- Write a closed question that will give you more information about levels of poverty in Whitechapel.
- Select a specific contemporary source that will have the answer to your question.
- Explain how your source will answer your question.

Glossary

abolition the act of ending a practice or punishment

beat constable a police officer whose duty is to walk 'the beat'. They patrol local areas to look for crime and act as a visual deterrent to those considering committing crime

benefit of clergy gave the accused the advantage of having their case heard at the more lenient church court if they could prove they were a member of the clergy

Bloody Code harsh laws introduced in the late seventeenth and eighteenth centuries that increased the number of crimes punishable by death

capital punishment the death penalty

conscientious objector a person who for reasons of conscience refuses to actively fight for the military during times of war

corporal punishment a physical punishment designed to inflict pain

crime against authority a crime which threatens or opposes the king, government or leaders

crime against the person a crime in which direct physical harm or force is used against a person

crime against property a crime which is carried out against personal property, such as a home or physical possessions.

Criminal Investigation Department (CID) a department in the police force that employs detectives to investigate crimes

deterrent/deterrence an act (often a punishment) which discourages or scares others into not committing crime

drug crime the crime of possessing, consuming, selling or smuggling illegal drugs

fine an amount of money paid as compensation for the crime committed

Forest Laws laws introduced by William I which designated protected forest land in which people could not hunt or gather wood

heresy the crime of holding religious beliefs different from those of the monarch

highway robbery stopping a stage coach on its journey and robbing the passengers

hue and cry raising the alarm (by shouting) when a crime was committed. Everyone within hearing distance was expected to join the hunt for the suspect

hundred the division of land (in an Anglo-Saxon shire) into approximately 100 households

immigrant a person who comes to live in another country permanently

justices of the peace men who upheld the law within their local area

maiming the act of wounding a person so that the part of their body is permanently damaged

migrants people who move from one place to another in search of work or better living conditions

Neighbourhood Watch an organisation set up in the early 1980s to prevent crime in local communities

non-custodial alternatives punishments which are used as an alternative to time in prison, such as an electronic tag

Norman Conquest the military conquest of England by William, Duke of Normandy, in 1066

open prisons prisons for low-risk category prisoners. They allow prisoners freedoms such as day release and work placements within the community

parish constables local people who helped to keep the peace and arrest criminals. Responsible for leading the hue and cry

penal reform the process of changing/improving punishments, including conditions in prisons

poaching the illegal hunting of animals

prevention the act of stopping something from happening

protection racket a system of taking money from people in exchange for agreeing not to hurt them or damage their property

public execution the act of carrying out capital punishment (the death penalty) in public as a deterrent to others

race crime crime which is motivated by racial prejudice

reform to make changes to something in order to improve it

retribution a punishment meant to match the severity of the crime committed

sanctuary a safe place within a church. Once a suspect claimed sanctuary, they could not be removed by force

scapegoat a person who is blamed for the mistakes or misfortunes of others

separate system a measure used in prisons to keep prisoners separated from one another. This prevented those who had committed serious crimes from mixing with lesser criminals and gave them a chance to reflect on what they had done

slum areas areas of housing which are considered to be unhealthy and/or dangerous

smuggling bringing goods into the country illegally

tithings groups of ten men who were responsible for each other's behaviour. If a member of the tithing broke the law, then the others had to bring them to justice or face a fine

Tolpuddle Martyrs six agricultural workers who were convicted of swearing a secret oath in 1834 after asking for better working conditions. The men were transported to Australia as punishment

town watchmen men who patrolled the streets to deter crime. They had powers of arrest and often dealt with vagabonds and drunks

transportation sending convicted criminals overseas as punishment

treason disobedience or disloyalty to the monarch or government

trial by ordeal a trial held by the Church in which God judged the accused with a sign of guilt or innocence

vagabondage the crime of wandering without a home or a job. Also known as vagrancy

Wergild a form of compensation paid to the victims of crime in Anglo-Saxon England

witchcraft the crime of using magic to cause harm to a person or their property

young offenders people under the age of 18 who have committed crime

INDEX

Barrett, Michael 50
benefit of clergy 20, 25, 39
Bentley, Derek 95, 96–7
Bloody Code 41, 54, 65, 71–2
Bloody Sunday 120–21
Booth, Charles 105, 110, 115, 120
borstal system 92, 93
Bow Street Runners 59

Catesby, Robert 30, 42, 43
Charles II 39, 52
Church: and law enforcement 19, 20, 24–5, 39
City of London police 120, 127
Clarke, Elizabeth 44–5
Clerkenwell bombing 50
collective responsibility 15, 18, 20, 24, 38
Community Protection Notices (CPNs) 91
conscientious objectors 98–9
courts 18, 20, 24, 25
   assizes 21, 38, 39
   quarter sessions 21, 39
   royal courts 21, 38
crime: definitions of 14, 16, 17, 31–2, 51, 52–6, 79
Criminal Behaviour Orders (CBOs) 91

demonstrations 122
DNA evidence 88
domestic violence 83
Doré, Gustave 109, 110
driving offences 84
drug crimes 84
drug smuggling 80, 81
drunkenness 23, 25, 40, 123
Du Cane, Edmund 70

Edward VI 34
Elizabeth I 33, 34, 39, 42
Ellis, Ruth 78, 95
Evans, Timothy 94

Fawkes, Guy 30, 42, 43, 81
Fielding, John and Henry 59, 60
fingerprinting 63, 88
food shortages 14, 32, 35, 44
Forest Laws 17, 23
Fry, Elizabeth 66, 67, 70, 90

Gunpowder Plot 30, 42–3

Harrying of the North 23
hate crime 82, 83
Henry II 21, 25
Henry VIII 31, 33, 34, 39
heresy 17, 31, 52
highway robbery 53, 59

Hopkins, Matthew (Witchfinder General) 44–5
housing 51, 106, 107, 108–14, 119, 123
Howard, John 66, 67, 90
hue and cry 19, 20, 21, 38, 58
human trafficking 80, 84

industrialisation 51, 52, 53, 58, 107
Irish immigrants 50, 115, 116–17, 121, 125
Irish Republican Brotherhood (Fenians) 50, 118, 121

Jack the Ripper murders 63, 123–5
James I 30, 34, 35, 42, 43, 81
Jewish immigrants 50, 118–19, 125
juries 18, 20, 21, 24, 65
justices of the peace (JPs) 21, 24, 38, 39

king's peace 18

Lawrence, Stephen 83
lodging houses (doss houses) 111, 116–17
London, Jack 112

Mearns, Andrew 109
Metropolitan Police Force 61–2, 63, 72, 83, 120–21, 122, 126, 127
Murdrum Law 16, 23

Neighbourhood Watch scheme 86

parish constables 21, 38, 39, 58
Patterson, Alexander 92
Peabody Estate 111
Peel, Robert 61, 65, 66, 71–2, 90
penal reform 66, 67, 71–2
people smuggling 80, 81
Peterloo Massacre 60
poaching 16, 17, 36, 55
Police Community Support Officers (PCSOs) 89
police 51, 59–63, 87–8
   City of London police 120, 127
   Metropolitan Police Force 61–2, 63, 72, 83, 118–19, 120, 123, 124
   Police Code 126
   science and technology 52, 63, 79–81, 87, 88–9
poverty 32, 33, 51, 52, 58, 60, 123
   poverty map 110, 119
   Whitechapel 107, 110, 111
prisons 40, 50, 65, 66, 67, 68–70, 90, 91
probation service 90, 91, 92, 93
punishment 14, 22–3, 40–1, 90–5
   capital punishment 17, 22, 23, 40, 94
   compensation 22, 23
   corporal punishment 17, 22, 23, 40

death penalty 34, 41, 50, 64, 65, 78, 94
   as deterrent 17, 22, 23, 40, 63
   fines 16, 22, 23, 40, 91
   hanging, drawing and quartering 23, 30, 40, 43
   humiliation 22, 23, 40
   as retribution 22, 23, 40

race crime 79, 82
racism 50, 83
restorative justice 91
retribution 22, 23, 40
Royal Society 52

sanctuary 25
separate system 68–9
smuggling 36, 54, 80–1
social crimes 16, 17, 36, 54, 80–1, 84
swim test 34, 45

taxes 36, 54, 60
terrorism 81
theft 16, 23, 31, 53, 80
Tolpuddle Martyrs 56–7
torture 30, 43, 45
trade unions 56–7
transportation 41, 56–7, 64–5
treason 16, 17, 23, 31
trial by ordeal 19

unemployment 33, 52, 60, 107

vagabondage 32–3, 40, 52
Van der Elst, Violet 78
Vincent, Howard 121, 126
violent crime 51, 53, 84, 123

Warren, Charles 120–21, 127
watchmen 21, 38–9, 58
Wergild 23
Whitechapel 50, 104–29
   crime 107, 123–5
   inhabitants 116–19
   local context 106–14
   maps 106, 110, 119
   national/regional context 120–21
   policing in 122–5
   prostitution 124
   rookeries 108, 113, 123
   sources 104–5
Whitechapel Vigilance Committee 125
William I 14, 16, 20, 23, 81
witchcraft 34–5, 44–5, 52
workhouses 33, 112–14

youth detention centres 92, 93